More
Nitty-Gritty
Grammar

More Nitty-Gritty Grammar

Another Not-So-Serious Guide to Clear Communication

by Edith H. Fine and Judith P. Josephson

TEN SPEED PRESS
Berkeley

Art credits:
    Momma by Mell Lazarus, *One Big Happy* by Rich Detorie, and *Rubes* by Leigh Rubin are reprinted with permission of the artists and Creators Syndicate, Inc.
    Baby Blues by Rick Kirkman and Jerry Scott, *Beetle Bailey* by Mort Walker, *Blondie* by Dean Young and Denis Lebrun, *Crock* by Bill Rechin and Don Wilder, *Mutts* by Patrick McDonnell, *Sally Forth* by Greg Howard, *Sherman's Lagoon* by Jim Toomey, *Six Chix* by Kathryn Lemieux, and *Zits* by Jerry Scott and Jim Borgman are reprinted with special permission of King Features Syndicate.
    9 Chickweed Lane by Brooke McEldowney (pp. 17, 35, 30, 45, 124, 152, 165) © 1998, 1998, 2000, 1998, 2000, 1998, 2000 by Los Angeles Times; *Against the Grain* by Glenn Foden (p. 89) © 1998 by Los Angeles Times; and *Single Slices* by Peter Kohlsaat (pp. 75, 206) © 2000 and 1998 by Los Angeles Times. Reprinted with permission.
    Jeff MacNelly's Shoe by Chris Cassatt and Gary Brooking and *Mother Goose and Grimm* by Mike Peters, copyright Tribune Media Services, Inc. All rights reserved. Reprinted with permission.
    Committed by Michael Fry, *Dilbert* by Scott Adams, *Drabble* by Kevin Fagan, *For Better or for Worse* by Lynn Johnston, *Frank & Ernest* by Bob Thaves, *Get Fuzzy* by Darby Conley, *Jump Start* by Robb Armstrong, and *Marmaduke* by Brad Anderson are reprinted with permission by United Feature Syndicate, Inc.
    Bizarro © by Dan Piraro, *Calvin and Hobbes* © by Watterson, *In the Bleachers* © by Steve Moore, *Non Sequitur* © by Wiley Miller, *Real Life Adventures* © by GarLanco, and *The Fusco Brothers* © by Lew Little Enterprises. Reprinted with permission of Universal Press Syndicate.
    B.C. by Johnny Hart and *Wizard of Id* by Brant Parker and Johnny Hart are reprinted by permission of Johnny Hart and Creators Syndicate, Inc.
    The Far Side © 1993 by Farworks, Inc. All rights reserved.
    Sylvia © by Nicole Hollander. Reprinted with permission of Nicole Hollander.

Library of Congress Cataloging-in-Publication Data
Fine, Edith Hope.
    More nitty-gritty grammar: another not-so-serious guide to clear communication / by Edith H. Fine and Judith P. Josephson.
        p. cm.
    Includes index.
    1. English language—Grammar.   I. Josephson, Judith Pinkerton. II. Title.
    PE1112 .F534 2001   428.2—dc21   2001004601

ISBN: 978-1-58008-228-0 (pbk.)

Printed in the United States of America

Cover and text design by Susan Van Horn

14 13 12 11 10 9 8 7
First Edition

Dedication

To all who love language and words.

Acknowledgments

Thanks to our eagle-eyed readers: Hilary Crain,
Teri Feldott, Janelle Fine, Michael Fine, Nick Genovese,
Jill Hansen, Beverly Hamowitz, Pat Hatfield, Melissa
Irick, Kirsten Josephson, Julianne Noll, Jeannie Phelan,
and Kay Vaughan.

We also tip our Grammar Patrol hats to editor
Meghan Keeffe and to our writing group for their
steady support and quick wit.

You Need Nitty-Gritty Grammar If . . .

▶ You worry that your participle might be dangling.

▶ You'd rather cover yourself in honey and roll in a mound of fire ants than think about grammar.

▶ You sing "Schoolhouse Rock" songs to remember what a conjunction is.

▶ You think TV newscasters are right when they say "nuCUEler" for "nuclear."

▶ You're never sure whether it's "it's" or "its."

▶ You're a CEO, and your mom still corrects your grammar.

▶ Your grammar checker makes your monitor glow green.

▶ You have an irrational fear of serial commas.

▶ You only read books with pictures. (Hey! This one has cartoons!)

▶ Your grammatically correct dog refuses to "lay down."

CONTENTS

CONTENTS

INTRODUCTION

Good communication is as stimulating as black coffee,
and just as hard to sleep after.

—Anne Morrow Lindbergh

"What? More grammar?" people asked when they heard we were writing
More Nitty-Gritty Grammar. "What's left to say?"

Our answer was "plenty."

Wearing our Grammar Patrol hats, we've appeared as guests on over
one hundred radio talk shows since our first grammar guide, *Nitty-Gritty
Grammar,* was published. It's been fun fielding questions and listening
to people's grammar pet peeves, such as "irregardless" and "between you
and I." We'll do anything to promote great grammar, including hauling
our four-foot-high Grammar Bear with us. While we chatted with "Money
in the Morning" radio host, George Chamberlin, the bear kept an eye on
the stock quotes.

Be assured that people across the United States and Canada really
do care about grammar and language. At KCET in Pasadena, California,
host Larry Mantle warned his eager listeners to pull off the freeways before
calling in with their grammar gripes. With all this great feedback and
fodder, our mission was clear: to write a follow-up book.

More Nitty-Gritty Grammar offers a painless language brush-up with a
comic bent, complete with a bevy of new syndicated cartoons. It's for anyone wanting to refresh, review, or polish grammar skills. Besides digging
deeper into topics lightly covered in our first book, we have stretched the
strict definition of "grammar" to include usage, literary terms, spelling, and
selective style pitfalls.

Both of our grammar books are designed for anyone from 10 to 110.
They are indispensable tools for busy executives and other businesspeople,
families, English teachers, second-language learners, graduates, and students
of all ages. As avid cartoon buffs, the Grammar Patrol appreciates all the
cartoonists who slip grammar jokes into their work. So, by popular request,
we've included over fifty new grammar cartoons by syndicated artists.

We wrote this second grammar guide to explore some finer points of
grammar and language, to further demystify grammar, to offer practical
suggestions, and to help readers increase their grammatical accuracy. We

also wanted to use the many real-life errors from our Blooper Patrol collection. But our most important goal was to serve up easy-access grammar basics, with dollops of laughter on the side.

Edith H. Fine and Judith P. Josephson
Encinitas, California

COMMITTED by Michael Fry

USING THIS BOOK

Here's a road map to help you travel easily through *More Nitty-Gritty Grammar,* whether you stick with the main highways or take shortcuts or detours.

Pop Quiz!

Uh-oh! On page 5, there's a pop grammar quiz. Where do you stand with grammar? Take this quick quiz and see. All the answers are in this book.

A to Z Format

More Nitty-Gritty Grammar has alphabetical listings, so you can go directly to the topic you want. For instance, to learn more about ending sentences with prepositions, look under "P" for "Prepositions," then find the "To End or Not to End?" header. You can read this guide page by page, or simply browse.

Ticker Tape

The all-new ticker tape that runs along the bottom of each page will look familiar to readers of our first grammar guide. These sentences highlight bloopers frequently seen and heard. You can treat the ticker tape as a quick refresher. If you say, "I don't get this," turn to the page number given in parentheses.

Right, Wrong, Why?

Nitty-Gritty Grammar veterans will also recognize the right-wrong-why icons—"Thumbs Up," "Thumbs Down," and "Why?"—that highlight frequent grammatical bloopers. Test your grammar savvy by comparing the right sentence with the wrong one, then read the "Why?" to understand the rule.

Terms and Headers

Grammarspeak We've used "Grammarspeak" to label proper grammatical terms, such as phrasal verbs, nonrestrictive clauses, and pronoun reference. Our less formal explanations will help you remember these terms and what they mean.

Substandard English Some words and phrases are labeled "substandard." "Substandard" means nonstandard English. When a dictionary labels a word "substandard," you should avoid using it in formal English (in business proposals and presentations, research papers, etc.). "Looking to," "get ahold of," "a whole nother," and "ain't," for example, are considered substandard for formal writing or speaking. But the Grammar Patrol itself has been known to say casually, "Ain't it the truth?" and "That's a whole nother ball game."

The Big E Alas, English grammar is riddled with exceptions to the rules. To draw attention to these exceptions, we have highlighted them. Be on the lookout for the label "THE BIG E," the exceptions.

Tips Grammar suggestions, mnemonics, and strategies are listed under "TIPS."

Did You Know? Under "DID YOU KNOW," we've included quirks, oddities, and interesting facts about our fascinating English language.

Mnemonic (Memory Aid) Memory aids, called mnemonics, can help jog your memory. These entries give rhymes, images, and ideas that will help you remember grammar terms, rules, or information.

Index

If you don't find a specific idea you're looking for in the A to Z listing, check the index.

Cartoons and Humor

Throughout the book, you'll find cartoons and funny examples, a lighthearted way to learn or review specific grammar points.

GET FUZZY by Darby Conley

Bucky, the irascible cat, doesn't quite get "the grammar thing." As usual, he's trying to blame his fractured spelling, grammar, and syntax problems on Satchel, the hapless dog. (Will anyone buy Bucky's "gud-smelling" fish heads: "no body, just heads"?)

UH-OH! A POP QUIZ! ABOUT GRAMMER!*

This pop quiz is also a sneak preview of what's to come. Look for answers to these bloopers within the pages of this book.

1. Let's divide these chocolates between you and _____.
   a. I
   b. me

2. Liver is different _____ filet mignon.
   a. than
   b. from

3. Leona has _____ baubles than Ivana does.
   a. fewer
   b. less

4. "_____ down, Satchel!" yelled Bucky.
   a. Lie
   b. Lay

5. _____ I said, my sweetie's no Romeo.
   a. As
   b. Like

6. Leonardo and _____ took a cruise.
   a. I
   b. me

7. Traffic is looking _____ on the freeway.
   a. badly
   b. bad

8. The champagne has lost _____ fizz.
   a. it's
   b. its

9. An orangutan's more _____ than a baboon.
   a. hairy
   b. hairier

10. The sanitation engineer watched the _____ turn to sludge.
    a. affluent
    b. effluent

11. Knees knocking, the groom approached the _____.
  a. alter
  b. altar

12. _____ now entering the state of Illinois.
  a. Your
  b. You're

13. I should have _____ you my Vikings tickets.
  a. gave
  b. given

14. The gerbil _____ behind the stove.
  a. snuck
  b. sneaked

15. Who authorized _____ running off to Rio?
  a. his
  b. him

16. "Help! I'm stuck in the _____ yelled Santa Claus.
  a. chimney,"
  b. chimney",

Stumped? See below for the quiz answers.
  * "Grammar" has two **a**'s. You get two A's if you caught the misspelling of "grammar" at the top of page 5!

Pop Quiz Answers: 1. b, 2. b, 3. a, 4. a, 5. a, 6. a, 7. b, 8. b, 9. a, 10. b, 11. b, 12. b, 13. b, 14. b, 15. a, 16. a

A NITTY-GRITTY GRAMMAR REFRESHER

Words do specific jobs in sentences to create meaning.

Verbs are the engines that power sentences. Without a verb, a sentence goes nowhere. Verbs show action or express a state of being.

> The space shuttle *Voyager* **blasted** into space.
> *(action)*

> Sicily **was** in New York City at last!
> *(state of being)*

Nouns are namers. Nouns name persons, places, things, or ideas.

> The stunning **soprano** took eight curtain **calls**.
> *(person)*   *(thing)*

> Ms. Jacobs's **charisma** draws students to her **classroom**.
> *(idea)*   *(place)*

Pronouns are substitutes. Pronouns take the place of nouns. For . . .

> **Secretariat** won racing's triple crown.
> *(noun)*

you can substitute . . .

> **He** won racing's triple crown.
> *(pronoun)*

Prepositions are locators. Prepositions can show position or time. They can also compare or connect.

> Besotted with his neighbor, Gladstone scrambled **over** the fence.
> *(preposition)*

> Norman Rockwell painted portraits **of** Americana.
> *(preposition)*

Adjectives are describers. Adjectives describe or modify nouns or other adjectives.

> The bride wore **black** boots under her gown.
> *(adjective)*

Adverbs are also describers. Adverbs modify verbs, telling *how, when,* or *where.*

> Vincent eased **gratefully** into his Barcalounger.
> *(adverb—how)*

> "That's it! I'm leaving for Fiji **tomorrow**!" yelled Horace.
> *(adverb—when)*

> The bear lumbered **forward**.
> *(adverb—where)*

Adverbs can also modify adjectives or other adverbs.

> The starlet's costume seemed **barely visible**.
> *(adverb) (adjective)*

> Mrs. Fezziwig danced **very lightly**.
> *(adverb) (adverb)*

Interjections are outsiders. They aren't official parts of a sentence. Interjections show feelings.

> **Okay, okay**. I'll take out the trash.
> *(mild interjection)*

> **Zoinks!** I'm off to the *Li'l Abner* tryouts.
> *(strong interjection)*

Conjunctions are connectors. Conjunctions join words or parts of a sentence.

> Sushi isn't sushi without ginger **and** wasabi.
> *(conjunction)*

> I studied entomology **because** my boyfriend's a bug nut.
> *(conjunction)*

GRAMMAR A TO Z

ABBREVIATIONS *(See acronyms, page 14, and initialisms, page 101.)*

DILBERT by Scott Adams

Abbreviations are shortened versions of words, such as "tsp." for "teaspoon." While some abbreviations still require periods, the periods have been dropped from others, especially the names of many organizations. Some abbreviations—called acronyms—can be pronounced as a word, such as "NATO" for North Atlantic Treaty Organization. Others—called initialisms—are read letter by letter, such as "AAUW" for the American Association of University Women.

When a sentence ends with an abbreviation that includes periods, use only one period.

Abbreviations are used frequently in parenthetical citations, notes, and bibliographies. Use them as little as possible in the text of your writing. Use only abbreviations that are easily understood by your readers. The first time you use an abbreviation, write out what it stands for, with the abbreviation in parentheses.

Check a recent dictionary when using abbreviations.

A.D. or **A.D.** (with or without periods) The abbreviation "A.D." is from the Latin *anno Domini*, meaning "in the year of the Lord." The A.D. goes before the year: A.D. 1066, A.D. 2010. Use small caps (small capital letters: A.D.), if possible. Otherwise, use regular capital letters. (*See also* B.C.)

Let's finish the croquet match. (*Not*, **Lets**—see page 109.)

a.m. or **A.M.** The abbreviation "a.m." stands for the Latin *ante meridiem,* which means "before noon." Use it for the time period between midnight and noon. Use "a.m." with numerals: 4:45 a.m. Don't use it with words: Instead of "five a.m.," write "five in the morning." You can choose whether to use lowercase letters or small caps (small capital letters: A.M.); just be consistent. (While most stylebooks show A.M. with periods, some allow AM without the periods.)

B.C. or **B.C.** (with or without periods) The abbreviation "B.C." means "before Christ." In naming a specific year, the B.C. goes after the year: 274 B.C.

cc The abbreviation "cc" used to stand for "carbon copy." Used after the signature in business letters, it indicates copies sent to others. Today, carbon copies are outmoded. Grammar Lady Mary Bruder suggests that "cc" can stand for "courtesy copy."

cf. or **cf** The abbreviation "cf." means "compare." Shown with one reference, it tells you to go to another source and compare the two.

d. The abbreviation "d." can stand for many words, such as "date," "day," "degree," and "departure." When used for "died," write "**d.** June 29, 1997."

e.g. The abbreviation "e.g." is from the Latin *exempli gratia* ("for the sake of example"). Think of it as "for example." Use "e.g." to list specific examples, not to explain or clarify a term or point. When using "e.g.," put a comma before and after. Use "e.g." only in citations and notes.

Study Chapter 1: simple machines, **e.g.**, levers, screws, and wedges.

et al. The abbreviation "et al." means "and others" and is used only in bibliographic entries and footnotes: Runsford, Truman, Jurgin, et al. (Do not put a period after "et": It's the Latin word for "and," not an abbreviation.)

etc. The abbreviation "etc." is from the Latin *et cetera,* meaning "and so forth." Since "et" means "and," don't write "and etc." Use "etc." sparingly in memos or technical writing when you mean "more of the same." (Say "**et** cetera," not "**eck** cetera.")

Right
Car racers face hurdles, **such as** turns, speed, and pit stops.

Wrong
Car racers face hurdles, **such as** turns, speed, and pit stops, **etc.**

She and I are going to the tattoo parlor. (*Not,* **Me and her**—see page 148.)

? **Why?** Don't use "etc." after a series that begins with "such as."
That's redundant.

ff The abbreviation "ff" (no periods) means "and the following." Use "ff"
only in citations and notes. (In music, the dynamic marking "ff," *fortissimo,*
means "play very loudly.")

> Newt reproduction, pages 134 **ff**, biology textbook

ibid. (pronounced "ib´ id") The Latin abbreviation "ibid." means "in the
same book or passage." "Ibid." is still sometimes used in citations and footnotes when an entry is from the same source as the one cited just before it.
But it is better and clearer to repeat the source by author or title. (Footnote
styles differ. Choose one stylebook and follow it consistently. See More
Grammar Resources, page 210.)

> Conroy, Pat. *The Water Is Wide* (New York: Bantam Books, 1972),
> page 43.
>
> **Ibid.,** page 87. (This cites *The Water Is Wide,* but a different page
> number.)
> > *or*
>
> Conroy, Pat. *The Water Is Wide* (New York: Bantam Books, 1972),
> page 43.
>
> Conroy, Pat. *The Water Is Wide,* page 87.

i.e. The abbreviation "i.e." is from the Latin *id est,* meaning "that is."
Use "i.e." to explain or clarify, not to give an example. Put a comma before
and after "i.e."

> The 30-meter three-legged dash was the penultimate race, **i.e.,** the
> second to last.

m. or **M.** The abbreviation "m." is from the Latin *meridies,* or "noon."

> 12:00 **m.** means noon
>
> 12:00 **P.M.** means midnight

The abbreviation "m." can also stand for "month," "Monday," and
other words.

Ms. or **Ms** (pronounced "miz") "Ms." is the widely accepted courtesy title
for women; like "Mr.," "Ms." doesn't indicate marital status.

These kinds of truffles are dangerously good. (*Not,* **These kind**—see page 154.)

n. The abbreviation "n." can stand for many words, such as "born," "noun," "noon," "north," and "number." When used for "born," it is from the Latin *natus:* **n.** January 6, 1913.

n.b. The abbreviation "n.b." stands for the Latin *note bene,* meaning "note well." It alerts your reader to take special note of information.

> **n.b.** Volatility could affect your earnings.

op. cit. The abbreviation "op. cit." stands for the Latin *opere citato:* "in the work cited." You will still sometimes see "op. cit." in citations and footnotes to refer to a book already cited, but it's more clear to use a shortened title instead. Include the author's name.
First footnote entry for a book by this author:

> Armstrong, Lance. *It's Not About the Bike: My Journey Back to Life* (New York: G.P. Putnam's Sons, 2000), pp. 105–108.

A later footnote entry for the same book by this author:

> Armstrong, *It's Not About the Bike*, page 88. (This refers to page 88 in *It's Not About the Bike.*)

TIP: Don't use "op. cit." if you have footnotes from two different books by the same author. Your reader won't know which book you mean.

p., pp. The abbreviation "p." stands for "page"; "pp." stands for "pages." Use only in citations, notes, and bibliographies. Don't use "pg." or "pgs.," even if your word processor tries to insist.

p.m. or **P.M.** The abbreviation "p.m." stands for the Latin *post meridiem:* "after noon." Use it to show the period of time between noon and midnight. (*See a.m.*)

PS The abbreviation "PS" stands for *postscript.* (Use no periods.) Use it for an additional thought at the end of a letter.

> **PS** Your check's in the mail. Really.

vs. or **vs** The abbreviation "vs." stands for "versus": UCLA Bruins vs. USC Trojans. But in most cases, use the word "versus," rather than the abbreviation.

> *Gladiator* was a movie about good **versus** evil. (In the language of law, a single "v." is used for "versus": Brown **v.** the Board of Education.)

As I said, Travis rescued Stella. (*Not,* **Like I said**—see page 37.)

ACCENT MARKS

Accent marks, called diacritical marks, are used to help with pronunciation. Here are the most common:

acute accent (´) tells you that the last syllable of certain words, especially those borrowed from French, is not silent. Thus, the noun "résumé" (ray´ zoo may)—a record of education and achievements—is distinguished from the verb "resume" (reh zoom´): to start again or restart. (In French, this mark is called *l'accent aigu.*)

grave accent (`) indicates pronunciation in French words, such as *chère.* "Grave" can rhyme with "pave" or be said with an "ah" sound, "grahv." This French pronunciation (the latter) is heard less frequently.

cedilla (seh dil´ eh) is a *c* with a squiggle below it: ç. It lets you know that the *c* is soft, sounding like an *s,* as in "façade" and "garçon."

circumflex (^) goes over a vowel to indicate a certain quality of sound: crêpes, tête-a-tête.

tilde (~) (teel´ deh) tells you to touch your tongue to the roof of your mouth to create an "enyuh" sound as you say words like "señora" or "mañana."

Marks specific to dictionary pronunciation are also handy to know:

macron (‾) (may´ kron) shows that a vowel is long. "Kite" looks like this: kīt.

breve (˘) tells you to use the short vowel sound. So "cat" looks like this: căt. ("Breve" can be pronounced two ways: to rhyme with "leave" *or* like the first syllable of "heaven.")

umlaut (¨) indicates a specific pronunciation (especially in Germanic languages): *über,* which means "all" in German, and *väggklocka,* for "wall clock" in Swedish, for instance.

Dictionaries have pronunciation guides to help you decipher these diacritical marks.

She told Steve and **me** about her cliff-plunge adventure (*Not,* **I**—see page 149.)

ACRONYMS *(See initialisms, page 101.)*

Acronyms are abbreviations formed by using the first letter or first few letters of a series of words. Acronyms are pronounced as words—for instance, SEALs = the Navy's **se**a, **a**ir, **l**and team. (By contrast, initialisms are pronounced letter by letter.) Some acronyms have become words and are spelled with lowercase letters. Here are three:

> **radar** = "**ra**dio **d**etecting **a**nd **r**anging"
> **scuba** = "**s**elf-**c**ontained **u**nderwater **b**reathing **a**pparatus"
> **laser** = "**l**ight **a**mplification by **s**timulated **e**mission of **r**adiation"

Most acronyms, though, are spelled with all capital letters and seldom have periods:

> **AIDS** = **a**cquired **i**mmuno**d**eficiency **s**yndrome
> **MADD** = **M**others **A**gainst **D**runk **D**riving
> **NATO** = **N**orth **A**tlantic **T**reaty **O**rganization
> **NASA** = **N**ational **A**eronautics and **S**pace **A**dministration
> **UNICEF** = **U**nited **N**ations **I**nternational **C**hildren's **E**mergency **F**und
> **WHO** = **W**orld **H**ealth **O**rganization
> **PIN** = **p**ersonal **i**dentification **n**umber
> **WYSIWYG** (Say, "wizzywig") = "**W**hat **y**ou **s**ee **i**s **w**hat **y**ou **g**et!"

ADJECTIVES *(See phrasals, page 130.)*

Adjectives are describers. They describe or modify nouns or other adjectives.

delicious cake	**high-tech** job	**blue** kite
sad song	**broken** mirror	**unending** curiosity

MOMMA by Mell Lazarus

Compound Adjectives *(See hyphens, page 91, and phrasal adjectives, page 131.)*
When two or more related words work together to describe a noun, they form a compound adjective, known in Grammarspeak as a "phrasal adjective."

Sergeant Pepper will take **roll call**. (*Not*, **role call**—see page 90.)

Compound Adjectives before Nouns

If a compound adjective comes before the noun, use a hyphen.

full-time work

Co Lee, a **24-year-old** pop vocalist

our **around-the-world** airfares

the **lime-green** VW Bug

an **over-the-top** concept

TIP: Keep the compound adjective and its noun separate. Don't use a hyphen right before the word being modified.

NASA hesitates to overemphasize its **life-on-Mars** card. (*Not,* **life-on-Mars-card**.)

Compound Adjectives after Nouns

After the noun, don't use a hyphen with compound adjectives.

Kofi Annan's U.N. **negotiations** were **high level**.

Cassie's **job** at WalMart is **full time**.

On Minnesota's KSTP radio, mosquito **reports** are **up to the minute**.

Compound Adjectives with Ethnicities

With compound ethnic adjectives or nouns, follow the "before" and "after" rules. If the compound adjective is before the noun it modifies, use a hyphen.

Vivian Lu is a **Chinese-American actress**.

When "Chinese American" is used as a noun, no hyphen is needed.

A **Chinese American** led the expedition.

Compound Adjective Exceptions

In addition to these reliable "before" and "after" rules, you may notice a baffling array of spellings for compound adjectives. Some always have spaces. Some always have hyphens. Some are always connected as single words. Wouldn't it be great if one rule covered all compound adjectives? Alas, none exists. In addition to the rules below, let a current dictionary or stylebook guide you.

Jessica's hunk detector works **well**. (*Not,* **good**—see page 19.)

Compound Adjectives Without Hyphens
Compound adjectives that don't have hyphens can be spaced or written as one word.

▶ Some compound adjectives have become so commonplace that they no longer need hyphens. A few examples:

> **life insurance policy**   **grand jury investigation**
> **income tax return**   **post office box**
> **lowest common denominator**

▶ Here are examples of one-word compound adjectives with no hyphen:

> **kindhearted uncle**   **Highland lassie**
> **statewide moratorium**   **halfhearted try**

Compound Adjectives with Hyphens
Some compound adjectives, like these, keep their hyphens, no matter where they fall in a sentence:

> **old-fashioned**   **air-conditioned**   **tailor-made**
> **soft-spoken**   **left-handed**   **time-consuming**

Adjective Pitfalls

▶ Resist the urge to use more adjectives than needed. They clutter your writing and distract your readers:

> Crystal thinks Bruno is **handsome, studly, and gorgeous.**

Try using one adjective that says it all:

> Crystal thinks Bruno is **gorgeous.**

▶ Be careful with "fun." The word "fun" used to be strictly a noun.

> Kirsten had **fun** at Moana's wedding.
>   *(noun)*

In casual speech, "fun" has turned into an adjective.

> Moana's wedding was **fun.** (Adjective: modifies noun "wedding.")

> **fun finger foods**   **fun little dress**   **fun time**

Some dictionaries now recognize "fun" as an adjective in informal speech and writing. Avoid "fun" as an adjective in formal speech and writing. Also avoid the comparative "funner," as in, "John's party was funner than Henry's."

Hugh wished his telephone **had rung.** (*Not,* **had rang**—see page 199.)

▶ Don't modifiy "unique." *(See comparisons, page 57.)*
The adjective "unique" means "one-of-a-kind," not "one of several." You can't make anything more "one of a kind." Since the Statue of Liberty is unique, it can't be "more unique," "so unique," or "very unique."

In Grammarspeak, "unique" is an "absolute adjective." It doesn't have degrees of comparison. Other absolute adjectives are "universal," "ideal," "main," and "final."

ADVERBS

9 CHICKWEED LANE by Brooke McEldowney

Adverbs are also describers. They modify verbs, adjectives, or other adverbs. Adverbs tell *how, when, where, why, how much,* or *to what extent.*

Aunt Blanche sews **beautifully**. (*How* does she sew? Beautifully.)

The incomparable Harry Belafonte performs here **tonight**. (*When* does he perform? Tonight.)

Adverb Pitfalls *(See advertising rule-breakers, page 21.)*

▶ Avoid using an adjective in place of an adverb.

 Wrong
Bridget Jones's Diary: A Novel did **tremendous**. (Should be the adverb "tremendously.")

 Wrong
The cartoon *Zits* shows that teens and adults think **different**. (Should be the adverb "differently.")

Tombstone Tour: $45, plus **guide's tip**. (*Not,* **guides tip** or **guides' tip**—see page 139.)

▶ Don't be fooled by *ly*.
Many adverbs end with *ly*. But some *ly* words are adjectives: *beastly, comely, costly, curly, friendly, growly, homely, pearly,* and *wobbly*.

a cost**ly** IPO

The Big Book of Beastly Pronunciations by Charles Harrington Elster

Some *ly* words can be adjectives *or* adverbs depending on how they are used.

The Iricks took a **leisurely** canoe ride. (Adjective: describes "ride.")

The Iricks paddled **leisurely** down the Fox River. (Adverb: tells how they paddled.)

ADJECTIVE, ADVERB PUZZLERS *(See adjectives, page 14, and adverbs, page 17.)*
Are you still confused about when to use adverbs and adjectives? Here's advice on other puzzlers:

Bad, Badly

▶ The adjective "bad" describes a noun or pronoun. It's the opposite of "good."

Comedian Robin Williams never has a **bad** night.

▶ The adverb "badly" describes a verb and tells "how" or "to what extent."

Right
The meeting went **badly** until the sword swallowers arrived.

Wrong
The meeting went **bad** until the sword swallowers arrived.

? **Why?** Use the adverb "badly" to show *how* the meeting went.

THE BIG E: With verbs of the five senses, use "bad," not "badly."
Things can **look bad, feel bad, sound bad, taste bad,** and **smell bad.**

I feel **bad** about dropping the pumpkin. (*Not,* **badly**.)

Ludmilla's Hungarian Goulash smelled **bad**. (*Not,* **badly**.)

Linda loves **lying** on the beach. (*Not,* **laying**—see page 194.)

Good, Well

▶ The adjective "good" describes a noun or pronoun.

Purple is not a **good** color for beards and mustaches.

▶ The adverb "well" describes the verb and tells *how*.

👍 **Right**
Mary Chapin Carpenter sang **well** at her concert.

👎 **Wrong**
Mary Chapin Carpenter sang **good** at her concert.

? **Why?** *How* did Mary sing? She sang **well**. The adverb "well" describes the verb "sang."

THE BIG E: With verbs of the five senses, use "good," not "well." Things can **look good, feel good, sound good, taste good,** and **smell good.**

Third quarter earnings look **good**.

The carne asada burrito tasted **good**.

Use "good" and "bad" with feelings, too. You wouldn't say "feel goodly" would you?

Olympic skater Joey Cheek should feel good about his donations.

Real, Really

MOMMA by Mell Lazarus

In informal speech, people often use "real" and "really" interchangeably. Actually, the two words do different jobs.

▶ "Real" is usually an adjective.

Is that a **real** Rolex watch? (Adjective: describes "Rolex.")

Miss Piggy **should have** run for president. (*Not,* **should of**—see page 191.)

► "Really" is usually an adverb.

> Marie **really** loves tap dancing. (Adverb: modifies the verb "loves."
> *How* does she love tap dancing? She *really* loves tap dancing.)

> These strawberries taste **really** good. (Adverb: modifies the
> adjective "good." *How* good do the strawberries taste? *Really* good.)

TIP: Overusing "really" can turn the word into a filler. (*See fillers, page 80.*)

> "There's Tanya, that **really** smart woman we **really** want
> to hire. **Really**!"

Cut some "reallys" and use stronger adverbs or adjectives.

> *The Fix:*
> "There's Tanya, that exceptionally bright woman we really hope to
> hire. She's perfect for the job."

Sure, Surely

► "Sure" is an adjective.

> The Rams' Marshall Faulk was a **sure** bet to win MVP in 2000.
> (Adjective: modifies the noun "bet.")

► "Surely" is an adverb.

> The pack mule walked **surely** down the steep trail.
> (Adverb: modifies the verb "walked.")

> **Surely** you jest!
> (Adverb: Modifies the verb "jest.")

In informal speech, you'll hear, "She **sure** likes iguanas." In professional
settings, avoid using "sure" for "surely."

Right
You **surely** made a great speech, Mayor Rodriguez.

Wrong
You **sure** made a great speech, Mayor Rodriguez.

Why? Think of "truly" for "surely." The adverb "surely" answers the
question "how?" *How* did he make the speech? *Surely* (or truly).

Ann **has written** a novel. (*Not,* **has wrote** or **has wroten**—see page 205.)

Usual, Usually

▶ "Usual" is an adjective.

> Detective Andy Sipowicz rounded up the **usual** suspects. (Adjective: describes "suspects.")

> TIP: The phrase "as usual" is an idiom, meaning "as commonly happens."

> **As usual**, we ate popcorn and Red Vines during the movie.

▶ "Usually" is an adverb.

> Dean Koontz **usually** writes suspense novels. (Adverb: modifies "writes" and answers the question "when?" *When* does he write suspense novels? *Usually.*)

Tight, Tightly

▶ "Tight" is an adjective. It describes a noun: a **tight** knot.

▶ "Tightly" is an adverb. It tells "how": coiled **tightly**.

THE BIG E: Some verbs suggest closing or constricting: *tie, close, hold, shut,* or *squeeze.* The word "tight" can follow such a verb and act as an adverb.

> **sit tight**   **hold tight**   **sleep tight**

ADVERSE, AVERSE

"Adverse" (ad´ verse) means "not favorable," while "averse" (uh verse´) means "reluctant or opposed."

> The guide canceled our kayak excursion due to **adverse** weather conditions.

> Because snails eat Chris's flowers, she is not **averse** to eating escargots.

ADVERTISING RULE-BREAKERS *(See adverb pitfalls, page 17; got, have, page 84; and homonyms, page 87.)*

Ad writers need pithy, colloquial expressions to make ads work. The goal is to create snappy messages that make a point and get people's attention. Advertising space is limited and costly, so ads must be catchy and clever, even if they break grammar rules. But sometimes, such ads make bloopers appear to be correct.

Cory and I use gargoyles for garden gnomes. (*Not,* **Cory and me**—see page 148.)

Adjective Rule-Breakers

Here are some examples of "ad speak":

Fly cheap!   **Drive slow!**   **Act quick!**

Technically, these should be adverbs—"cheaply," "slowly," "quickly"—because these words tell *how* to fly, drive, or act.

Headline: Cook **Organic**, Think **Holistic**.

"Organic" and "holistic" are adjectives. To modify "cook" and "think," you need adverbs that tell *how:* "organically" and "holistically."

Pronoun Rule-Breakers *(See pronouns, page 147.)*

Ad: My Happy Cow Ice Cream and **me** were alone.

"My Happy Cow Ice Cream and me" is a compound subject. Change the objective pronoun "me" to the subjective pronoun "I."

My Happy Cow Ice Cream and **I** were alone.

TIP: Omit "My Happy Cow Ice Cream and." You wouldn't say, "**Me** was alone." Say, "**I** was alone."

Punctuation Bloopers

Punctuation errors also abound in ad copy.

Ad: Best Doctor**'s** in the Business

"Doctors" is plural, not possessive. Don't use apostrophes to pluralize.

TV show: *Who Wants to Be a Millionaire*

A question mark should follow "Millionaire." It's a question, not a statement.

Ad: A **User Friendly** Web Site for Your Business

The compound adjective "User-Friendly" comes before the noun "Web Site." Use a hyphen.

ADVICE, ADVISE

"Advice" is a noun meaning "opinion or guidance." "Advise" is a verb meaning "to give or offer advice."

Alejandra needs your **advice** on raising orchids.

Ms. Linden **advised** the kindergarten parents to "read to your bunnies."

I **saw** the Doo-Dah Parade on *Oprah* yesterday. (*Not,* **seen**—see page 204.)

AFFECT, EFFECT

MUTTS by Patrick McDonald

"Affect" and "effect" have distinct meanings.

Affect

Think of "affect" as a verb when you mean "to influence."

> Pesticides negatively **affect** creatures living deep in the ocean.

> Did apathetic voters **affect** the election?

As a noun, "affect" is a term used by psychologists:

> Art's sad **affect** brightened when he heard, "Surprise! Happy birthday!"

(Emphasize the first syllable: af´ fekt.)

Effect

Think of "effect" as a verb when you mean "to bring about."

> The new CEO **effected** sweeping changes at Swizzlesticks.com.

As a noun, "effect" means "result."

> Hawaii's balmy climate has a relaxing **effect** on tourists.

(Say, "eh fekt´," not "ee´ fekt.")

MNEMONIC (MEMORY AID): "Affect" is usually a verb. "Effect" is usually a noun—remember the phrase "Now in effect." This sounds a lot like "noun-effect" and can help you remember "effect" for its job as a noun.

AFFLUENT, EFFLUENT

"Affluent" (af´ loo ent) means "financially comfortable," while "effluent"

There are not enough appetizers. (*Not,* **There is** or **There's** [there is]—see page 26.)

(ef' loo ent) is the liquid from waste pipes or sewers.

Shaker Heights is an **affluent** neighborhood.

Dead goldfish often enter the **effluent** stream by way of the toilet.

Don't switch these two words. Once, in a column about a wastewater treatment plant, an overly diligent copy editor incorrectly changed every "effluent" to "affluent," with startling results:

The **affluent** swished through the grates into the holding tank.

AGREEMENT *(See collective nouns, page 51; number, page 120; and person, page 130.)*

Spouses, opposing politicians, and other pairings don't always have to agree. (Fortunately!) But in the world of grammar, specific words must agree with other words. Here's how:

BIZARRO by Dan Piraro

Pronoun-Noun Agreement
(See nouns, page 118, and pronouns, page 147.)
Pronouns must agree in person (first, second, or third), number (singular or plural), and gender with the nouns they replace.

Former football star **Refrigerator Perry** likes **his** new job as a bricklayer.
                              (noun)   *(pronoun)*

👍 **Right**
Entertainers are performers. **They** play to the crowd.

👎 **Wrong**
An entertainer is a performer. **They** play to the crowd.

❓ **Why?** Pronouns must agree with their subjects. "Entertainers" is plural: "They" play. "An entertainer" is singular: "He" or "she" plays.

It's revolting! (*Not*, **Its**—see page 105.)

Pronoun-Antecedent Agreement

BLONDIE by Dean Young and Denis Lebrun

Which "she" is Dagwood's son talking about? Kelly or Britney? If your reader is confused by which person your pronoun stands for, you have—in Grammarspeak—a "pronoun reference problem." Be sure each pronoun you use refers to the closest noun before it.

A pronoun takes the place of a noun. The closest noun that comes before a pronoun is called its **antecedent**: literally, "what comes before." Pronouns must agree with their antecedents in person and number.

The world's Garlic Capital is **Gilroy, California**. You'll smell **it** miles away.
          (*singular noun*)   (*singular pronoun*)

The **guys** met **their** dates at the mixer.
  (*plural noun*)(*plural pronoun*)

Indefinite Pronoun–Pronoun Agreement (*See gender-inclusive language, page 83.*)

 Right
Everybody must build **his or her** own sand castle.

 Wrong
Everybody must build **their** own sand castle.

 Why? "Everybody" is singular, even though it may sound plural.

To agree, the pronoun following "everybody" must also be singular. If it's a co-ed sand castle event, use "his or her."

It used to be that the pronoun "his" covered both males and females. Today, people recognize the power of language and acknowledge females with the use of "his or her."

Another fix is to use plural nouns instead of indefinite pronouns.

All contestants must build **their** own sand castles.

You're our hero, President Carter. (*Not,* **Your**—see page 209.)

DID YOU KNOW? Some usage experts are also recognizing the plural "their" with the singular "everyone" and "everybody," as used in the wrong example above, to avoid the awkward "his or her." The Grammar Patrol recommends sticking with singular-singular or plural-plural forms for agreement.

Subject-Verb Agreement *(See predicate nouns, page 141.)*
Verbs must agree with their subjects in person and number.

Right
Teri **makes** awesome bacon pie.

Wrong
Teri **make** awesome bacon pie.

? **Why?** The subject, "Teri," is third person singular. To check which verb form to use, replace "Teri" with the pronoun "she." Say, "She makes." Add *s* to "make" in the third person singular form. (*See verbs, page 199*).

Right
The first Latin Grammy Awards **were** held in Los Angeles.

Wrong
The first Latin Grammy Awards **was** held in Los Angeles.

? **Why?** The subject, "Latin Grammy Awards" is plural. Use the plural verb "were" to match the plural "awards." If it were "Latin Grammy Awards ceremony," you'd use the singular "was" to match the singular "ceremony."

TIP: When a verb is hidden in a contraction, like "there's" (for "there is"), remember the rules of agreement. Don't say, "There's Popsicles in the freezer." That means, "**There is** Popsicles." Say, "There **are** Popsicles" (often shortened to "There're Popsicles" in casual speech). This applies to other contractions, such as "where's" for "where is."

Agreement with a Compound Subject
In sentences with a compound subject (two or more nouns joined by the conjunction "and"), the verb must be plural.

<u>Red, white, and blue</u> **are** the colors of the American flag. (*They* are.)

    (*compound subject*) (*plural verb*)

<u>Siegfried and Roy</u> **attract** huge crowds in Las Vegas. (*They* attract.)

    (*compound subject*) (*plural verb*)

Where is it? (*Not,* **Where's it at?**—see page 146.)

THE BIG E: If the compound subject is a thing or a unit, make the verb singular.

Romeo and Juliet is by William Shakespeare.

(compound subject) (singular verb)

(Why? *Romeo and Juliet* is one play. Use a singular verb.)

If you're puzzled about compound subjects joined by "or," see coordinating conjunctions, page 62.

ALLITERATION

Alliteration is the repetition of letters or sounds in words that are close together.

ten tall trumpeters　　　**classy, competent, and cool**

Effective in both poetry and prose, alliteration loses its allure with overuse.

Billy Bob bought beer for baseball buddies at Bubba's Bar.

ALLUDE, ELUDE

"To allude" is "to refer to indirectly." "To elude" is "to escape or avoid by daring or cunning."

The con artist **alluded** to riches to be gained from a hot new dot-com.

The cat burglar **eluded** the police.

ALTAR, ALTER

An "altar" (a noun) is a table used in religious ceremonies. "To alter" (a verb) is "to change or adjust."

The bride and groom cartwheeled away from the **altar**.

Who but Superman can **alter** the tide of fate?

AMONG, BETWEEN (See objective pronouns, page 148; phrasal verbs, page 131; and prepositions, page 143.)

Grammar guides used to call for using the preposition "between" with two people or things, and using the preposition "among" with more than two.

between dawn and dusk　　　**among** the four bass players

Frankenstein arrived with **him** and a werewolf. (*Not*, **he**—see page 149.)

While this rule is relaxing, do use "between" in one-to-one or direct relationships.

> Choose a number **between** six and fifteen.

> Oli's life is a balancing act **between** work and tae kwon do.

Use "among" when the relationship is less specific, broader.

> Divide the kumquats **among** the neighbors.

> **Among** the many descendants of Johann Sebastian Bach, four became musicians.

When using "between," which suggests two items, use "and," not "or," to connect the two words:

> My fiancé said I could choose **between** Fiji **and** Fargo for our honeymoon. (*Not,* **between** Fiji **or** Fargo.)

TIP: "Amongst" is out of date. Don't use "amongst" unless you are rewriting the Bible or some other ancient tome. (Likewise, avoid "whilst," "amidst," and "unbeknownst.")

AMOUNT, NUMBER (See *fewer, less, page 78.*)

The words "amount" and "number" are easily confused. Use "amount" when referring to a quantity. Use "number" with things you can count.

> After shoveling manure, Jasper needed a massive **amount** (*not* **number**) of cologne.

> Mike and Greg can eat a larger **amount** (*not* **number**) of mashed potatoes than Paul Bunyan.

> Tammy Belle had a **number** (*not* **amount**) of things to buy at the Piggly Wiggly.

> Unfortunately, Dudley had consumed a large **number** (*not* **amount**) of prunes.

AMPERSAND

Some people call the ampersand (**&**) the "fancy 'and.'" You see this symbol in names of companies, such as Lee **&** Low Books, Quick **&** Reilly, and Procter **&** Gamble. Names of law firms often include an ampersand and skip the serial comma: Olson, Noll **&** Drury. (There's also Dewey,

---

I **should have gone** bowling. (*Not,* **should have went**—see page 204.)

Cheetham **&** Howe, the infamous law firm touted by NPR's zany Car Guys, Click and Clack.)

In writing, don't use an ampersand as a shortcut for "and." The same goes for book titles. Write *Python **and** Anaconda,* not *Python **&** Anaconda.*

DID YOU KNOW? Ampersands won't work in either email or Internet addresses. For Internet access, Lee & Low Books becomes **www.leeandlow.com**. Barnes & Noble becomes **www.barnesandnoble.com**.

ANACHRONISM, ACRONYM *(See acronyms, page 14.)*

An anachronism (eh nak´ kro nizm) is a chronological error, a mismatch in time. It means an implausible event that usually refers to an earlier era, such as Cleopatra having a Web site or William the Conqueror hopping into his private jet.

An acronym is an abbreviation that can be said as a word: WAC for Women's Army Corps.

ANALOGY *(See metaphors, page 113, and similes, page 176.)*

Analogies compare objects or people, often with similar features. In speech or writing, analogies can help illustrate or describe.

Dr. Au made an analogy between a stomach and a food processor.

Beverly compared her high-strung client to a spirited racehorse.

AND, BUT

Remember the old grammar rule: "Never start a sentence with a conjunction"? Today, it's perfectly acceptable to begin sentences with "and," "but," or other conjunctions like "for," "or," or "nor," especially for quick emphasis. (No comma follows "and" or "but" when used at the beginning of a sentence.)

The Boston Pops's Keith Lockhart loves conducting. **And** it shows.

Painters don't dress up when they work. **But** why would they?

ANECDOTE, ANTIDOTE

An anecdote is a short tale about an event, often funny. An antidote relieves or counteracts.

Colleen entertains better than **I**. (*Not,* **me**—see page 156.)

👍 **Right**
Today, a crystal ball seems the only **antidote** to economic woes.

👎 **Wrong**
Today, a crystal ball seems the only **anecdote** to economic woes.

? **Why?** While the laughter of a funny tale ("anecdote") might cheer you up, don't try it as the remedy ("antidote") for your money troubles.

ANXIOUS, EAGER

"Anxious" means "worried or distressed." Think of the word "anxiety." "Eager" is "keenly interested, impatiently longing."

> I'm **anxious** about my test score. (worried)

> I'm **eager** to find out my test score. (keenly interested)

TIP: "Anxious" is usually followed by "for" or "about." "Eager" is usually followed by "to."

ANYWAY, ANYWAYS (See substandard words, page 185.)

"Anyway" means "in any case" or "in any way whatever." "Anyways" is substandard. Avoid it.

> I tried the rattlesnake meat **anyway**.

APOSTROPHES (See contractions, page 190, and possessives, page 137.)

9 CHICKWEED LANE by Brooke McEldowney

Are our children learning? (*Not*, Is—see page 26.)

Apostrophes (') do several jobs. Use apostrophes:

▶ To replace missing letters in contractions or surnames.

> **do + not = don't**
> **you + are = you're**
> **would + not = wouldn't**

Rosie O'Donnell is a champion for children's rights.
(The apostrophe replaces the letter *f* in "of"—"of Donnell.")

▶ To replace missing numerals or letters.

> The class of '05 [2005]

> Newspaper headline: "Ol' Coots Still Have Right Stuff in *Space Cowboys*"

▶ To show possession.
Nouns show possession or ownership with the addition of an apostrophe.

> an astronaut's view of earth

> Janelle's favorite flowers

DID YOU KNOW? The top two apostrophe bloopers are switching the pairs "it's" and "its" and "your" and "you're." "It's" and "you're" are contractions. "Its" and "your" are possessive pronouns.

Wrong
The Yacht Club held **it's** yearly regatta. (Should be the possessive "its.")

Wrong
Billboard: Slow down unless **your** planning to become a hood ornament. (Should be the contraction "you're," for "you are.")

▶ To form plurals of lowercase letters.

> **Mind your p's and q's.**   **Dot your i's and cross your t's.**

▶ To form plurals of abbreviations with periods or abbreviations formed with capitals if the meaning is unclear without the apostrophe.

> **M.A.'s**   **Ph.D.'s**   **SOS's**

(SOS would read "SOSs" without the apostrophe.)

The feisty jockey's nickname is "Spitfire." (*Not,* "Spitfire".—see page 165.)

DID YOU KNOW? It used to be that you routinely showed plurals of numbers and abbreviations with an apostrophe. Times are changing. Today, if the meaning is clear, the plurals of dates, numbers, and combinations of capital letters do not require an apostrophe, though some people do still use them.

Steam changed the world in the **1800s** (*not* **1800's**).

Save all **1099s** (*not* **1099's**) for preparing your income tax return.

We tried three **ATMs** (*not* **ATM's**).

Likewise, **IPOs**, **CEOs**, **JPEGs**, and **PDFs**.

Apostrophe Don'ts

▶ Do *not* use apostrophes to form plurals of nouns.

balloons (*not* **balloon's**)   the **Smiths** (*not* the **Smith's**)

▶ Do *not* use apostrophes to make pronouns possessive. (*See pronouns, Chart 3, page 149.*)

Resist the urge to slip apostrophes into pronouns just to prove you know that apostrophes are used to make nouns possessive.
Never use these forms:

her's	our's	it's
your's	their's	

Pronouns have specific forms that show possession: *my, your, her, his, its, our, their.* These are the correct possessive pronouns:

hers	**ours**	**its**
yours	**theirs**	

TIP: Beware! Don't ever write "its'." The apostrophe *never* goes at the end of "its."

Yours are the best photos of the shuttle liftoff.

I ordered the pickled beets—the oxtail omelette was **hers**.

I traded my car for **theirs**.

Take it from the Grammar Patrol. Do *not* put an apostrophe in the possessive word "its." "It's" is never a possessive pronoun. Use "it's" only when you mean the contraction "it is." We'll say it again, but this four-word mnemonic (memory aid) works: Possessive "**its**" never sp**lits**!

Florists take romance **seriously**. (*Not,* **serious**—see page 17.)

THE BIG E: Dare we mention one teensy exception? The pronoun "one" is indefinite, so you *do* add *'s* to show possession: one**'s**.

> When choosing a mate, one must hold to **one's** standards.

ONE LAST APOSTROPHE TIP: Ninety-nine percent of the time, you'll see apostrophes in contractions or to show possession. In *rare* cases, you use apostrophes to make nouns plural if your reader would be confused without the *'s*.

For instance, when you write the plural of "do and don't" as "dos and don'ts," the meaning of "dos" is clear—it's the plural of the word "do." But if the word "dos" appears alone and without the apostrophe, it could be confusing. It could be read as DOS (rhymes with "boss") for "disk operating system" or "dos" (rhymes with "shoes") for the plural of "do." When the word "dos" appears alone, an apostrophe makes it clearer: Jen and John said their "I **do's**" in February.

APPOSITIVES

Think of appositives as renamers: nouns or noun phrases that describe a noun or pronoun.

> Oscar de la Hoya, **boxing's singing Golden Boy**, has a match this Saturday.

The appositive "boxing's singing Golden Boy" describes, or renames, the proper noun "Oscar de la Hoya."

Nonessential Appositives

When appositives follow the noun or pronoun they describe, use commas to separate them from the rest of the sentence. Such appositives set off information that is not essential (nonessential) to the sense of the sentence. (In Grammarspeak, "nonrestrictive.")

> Kit Kat, **Andrea's beloved cat,** rules the house. (Kit Kat still rules the house, whether he belongs to Andrea or not.)

> Nikki Giovanni, **a highly regarded poet,** speaks at Harvard today.

You may also use em dashes or parentheses to set the appositive apart.

> Pearl—**the Koemptgens' pet squirrel**—stuffs peanuts in her cheeks.

> Montreal **(Canada's second largest city)** is cold in the winter.

Café Flour Power showcased **its** new torte. (*Not,* **it's**—see page 105.)

33

Essential Appositives

When the appositive restricts or limits the noun it renames, use no commas. These appositive phrases are needed (essential). They give specific meaning to the words they describe. Often, essential appositives come before the noun they are describing. (In Grammarspeak, these appositives are "restrictive": They restrict the meaning of the noun.)

The romantic comedy *Pretty Woman* made Julia Roberts famous.
   (appositive)   (noun)

The late blues singer Alberta Hunter sang that song.
   (appositive)   (noun)

The thriller movie *The Bone Collector* gave Marco nightmares.
   (appositive)   (noun)

Appositives with Family Names

The wicket gets stickier when it comes to family members. (Why aren't we surprised?) Let's assume you have three brothers.

My brother George adores artichokes.

If you just said, "My brother likes artichokes," without George's name, we wouldn't know which of your three brothers loves artichokes. (The information is essential, so there's no comma.)

Now, imagine you have one sister.

My sister, Betty, bakes great pumpkin pies.

You could say, "My sister bakes great pumpkin pies," without the word "Betty," because we know who you mean, even without her name. The name "Betty" is nonessential, so it's enclosed in commas. (If you had other sisters, you'd need to name the pumpkin pie expert: The name would be essential.)

APPRAISE, APPRISE

"To appraise" is "to set a value on." "To apprise" is "to inform."

Lou **appraised** the Lionel train sets.

The captain **apprised** the romance cruise passengers of rough seas ahead.

Ted and Tisha's van was stolen. (*Not,* Ted's and Tisha's—see page 138.)

ARTICLES (See *percent, percentage*, page 128.)

CHICKWEED LANE by Brooke McEldowney

The words "the," "a," and "an" are articles. They work as adjectives, modifying nouns. Their pronunciation changes depending on the word that follows the article.

The

"The" is a definite article: It points to a specific noun.

▶ Pronounce "the" as "thuh" before words that start with a consonant sound.

the ("thuh") theater

the ("thuh") Monopoly game

the ("thuh") beach ball

▶ Pronounce "the" as "thee" before words that start with a vowel sound.

the ("thee") inchworm

the ("thee") eight ball

the ("thee") honor (You hear the vowel sound of the *o*, not the unvoiced beginning *h*.)

the ("thee") Olympic games

A or An?

The words "a" and "an" are **indefinite articles**: They are general, not specific.

a hotel in France   an uncle

Bill's and Alma's tubas collided. (*Not,* **Bill and Alma's**—see page 138.)

► Use "a" before words or abbreviations that start with a consonant sound.

> a mango
> a kangaroo
> a historian (Pronounce the *h*.) (*See historic, historical, page 87.*)
> a Lexus
> a YMCA fund-raiser
> a ukulele (It starts with a "y" sound—a consonant.)

Pronounce "a" as "uh," unless you are emphasizing.

> "I said you could have **a** cookie!" shouted Jessica. (Jessica meant one cookie, not six. The **a** rhymes with "day.")

► Use "an" before words that start with a vowel sound.

an iMac	an umbrella	an ostrich egg
an attaché case	an August moon	an emperor penguin

Also use "an" with words beginning with a consonant that makes a vowel sound.

> **an** hour (You hear the vowel sound of the *o*, not the beginning *h*.)

With abbreviations, use "an" if the first letter has a vowel sound.

> **an** FBI agent (*but* **a** **F**ederal Bureau of Investigation agent)

> **an** NCTE member (*but* **a** **N**ational Council of Teachers of English member)

> **an** SASE (*but* **a** **s**elf-addressed stamped envelope)

> **an** RSVP card (*but* **a** **r**esponse card)

"A" and "The" before the Word "Number"
When the article "a" appears before the singular noun "number," use a plural verb.

> **A** number of Dallas Cowboys fans **have** season tickets. (*They* have.)
> (*article*) (*plural verb*)

When "the" appears before the word "number," use a singular verb.

> Shania Twain's new album is hot; **the** number sold **is** 26 million. (*It* is.)
> (*article*) (*singular verb*)

Sabah helps **whoever** calls. (*Not,* **whomever**—see page 155.)

AS, LIKE (See metaphors, page 113; prepositions, page 143; similes, page 176.)

Life is like a box of chocolates.

—Forrest Gump

"As" and "like" are both prepositions. They compare one thing to another, forming a simile. What follows "like" or "as" is the object of the preposition. "As" can also be a conjunction.

"As" and "Like" as Prepositions

glamorous **as** a **movie star**
  (preposition) (object of a preposition)

scary **as** a black widow **spider**
  (preposition)   *(object of a preposition)*

ugly **as** green **slime**
  (preposition) (object of a preposition)

fits **like** a **glove**
  (preposition) (object of a preposition)

sounded **like** a **politician**
  (preposition) (object of a preposition)

moves **like** a **dancer**
  (preposition) (object of a preposition)

"As" as a Conjunction

Besides working as a preposition, "as" plays another role: as a conjunction, a connector. When used as a conjunction, a clause, containing a subject and a verb, follows "as."

"Kick it up a notch!" says Emeril Lagasse **as he adds hot peppers**.
  (conjunction) (clause)

As the World Turns is Nan's favorite show.
(conjunction) (clause)

(In the show's title, "as" is a conjunction introducing the clause "the world turns.")

Dirk talked finances **as I trimmed his toenails**.
  (conjunction)   *(clause)*

The Lotto jackpot was **bigger** than expected. (*Not,* **more bigger**—see page 60.)

Don't use "like" as a conjunction.

Right
As I said, martial arts guru Billy Blanks is an exercise fanatic.

Wrong
Like I said, martial arts guru Billy Blanks is an exercise fanatic.

? Why? "As I said" is a clause that starts with the conjunction "as." "Like" is a preposition, not a conjunction: It can't introduce a clause. Instead, use "as."

TIP: Use the preposition "like" with nouns and noun phrases. Use the conjunction "as" with verbs and clauses. (Conjunctions introduce clauses, and clauses contain verbs.) Don't follow the preposition "like" with a verb. Instead of, "I voted **like** I did last time," say, "I voted **as** I did last time." Use "as" because the verb "did" follows it.

AS IF, AS THOUGH
"As if" and "as though" are interchangeable. Either phrase can signal that a clause follows.

Bill Cosby acted **as if he knew me**!
(clause)

It looks **as though juggling lessons are in your future**.
(clause)

TIP: The term "as if" can also usher in the subjunctive. (*See subjunctive mood, page 197.*)

Right
Trixie bought shoes **as if** she **were** Imelda Marcos.

Wrong
Trixie bought shoes **as if** she **was** Imelda Marcos.

? Why? Trixie is not the shoe-loving Imelda Marcos. Don't write "as if she **was**." Use the subjunctive "**were**."

ASTERISKS (*See bullets, page 44.*)
"Asterisk" is Greek for "little star." An asterisk (*) by a word, phrase, graph, or chart leads readers to additional information.

Your Pekingese terrifies my Rottweiler. (*Not,* **You're** —see page 209.)

> Stock ownership in home-repair companies
> has risen 7 percent yearly over the decade.*
> Do-it-yourselfers and "fixer" homes are the
> driving forces . . .

*With the exception of a 10 percent drop in 2001.

The trickiest thing about an asterisk is how to say it. Say, "aster" (like the flower) plus "isk," not "ick." "Aster-isk." Think, "risk an asterisk."

TIP: In advertising, contracts, and credit card agreements, asterisks often lead you to must-read (but often unreadable!) details found in the fine print.

ATTAIN, OBTAIN

"To attain" is "to accomplish or gain," or "to reach through time." "To obtain" is "to get or acquire."

> Tomás has **attained** the ultimate in wood-working accolades.

> To **obtain** entry to the estate, Jason had to get past four pit bulls.

A WHILE, AWHILE

Both "a while" and "awhile" mean "for a short time." The difference is easy. Use the single word "awhile" unless it follows a preposition—in that case, make it two: "a while."

> Let's chat **awhile.**

> Let's chat for **a while.**
> (preposition)

Where are my Ripplin' Red lures? (*Not,* **Where's** [where is]—see page 26.)

B

BESIDE, BESIDES

The preposition "beside" means "at the side" or "near."

> Kalie sat **beside** Bill at the Square Lake picnic.

The preposition "besides" means "also," "in addition to," "except for," or "other than."

> **Besides** her sister Brianna, Marissa has two brothers, Johnny and Mike.

BOLDFACE

Like electric green hair, boldface stands out. Avoid using boldface in everyday writing or regular text. Your words, not the typeface, should make your point. Graphic designers find boldface useful for mastheads, headlines, titles, headings, and subheadings.

Boldface can also make computer commands stand out.

> To force-quit a Macintosh application that appears to be frozen, press **command + option + escape**.

BOTH, EACH

The indefinite pronouns "both" and "each" can be used as adjectives or pronouns.

Both

"Both" applies to two people or things. Look for a plural verb with "both," whether it's an adjective or a pronoun.

> **Both** Steve Jobs and Donald Duck **like** bow ties. (*They* like.)
> (*adjective*)   (*plural verb*)

> When Leticia and Malik do aerobics, **both wear** sequins. (*They* wear.)
>   (*pronoun*) (*plural verb*)

Each

"Each" applies to one person or thing: Think "each one" or "every single one." When "each" is used as a pronoun, use a singular verb.

> **Each** Rose Bowl float **is** unique. (*It* is.)
> (*adjective*)   (*singular verb*)

It's time for Liz and **me** to build a snowman. (*Not,* I—see page 149.)

Each gets a Tootsie Roll. (*He or she* gets.)
(*pronoun*) (*singular verb*)

If the pronoun "each" appears after a plural noun, make the verb plural.

The Bearskin Lodge **cabins each have** a fireplace. (*They* have.)
(*plural noun*) (*pronoun*) (*plural verb*)

BOTH, EACH OTHER

Using the phrases "both" and "each other" in the same sentence is redundant. Instead of, "*Both* men congratulated *each other* on their fishing skills," say, "The men congratulated *each other* on their fishing skills."

 Right
Brian Williams mentioned **both** of you.

Wrong
Brian Williams mentioned **the both** of you.

? **Why?** Don't use the article "the" with "both."

BRACKETS (*See also italics, page 102.*)

Brackets ([ ]) enclose added information or an explanation. Use brackets:

▶ To enclose *sic*, meaning "thus" or "so." What *sic* tells the reader is, "this is not our error; it was written this way."

> The student wrote, "President Kennedy was assassinated in 1964 **[sic]**." (The correct year is 1963.)

> Sven's cat Mugsie prefers makral **[sic]** to anchovies. (Should be "mackerel.")

▶ To add omitted information in a direct quotation.

> "I'm building my Fairmont **[West Virginia]** mansion on Pinchgut Hollow Road," gushed Daisy May.

▶ To clarify.

> Westley told his true love **[Buttercup]**, "As you wish."

▶ To show parenthetical information inside parentheses.

> Fine and Josephson could only laugh when reviewers misspelled their first grammar title as *Nitty-Gritty Grammer*. (*Nitty-Gritty Grammar* **[Ten Speed Press, 1998]**).

Snails-to-Go is closing **its** doors forever. (*Not,* **it's**—see page 105.)

BRING, TAKE

We dedicate this section to Tom and Ray Magliozzi, NPR's venerable Car Guys, who dispense equal parts humor and automotive advice. "Bring" and "take" remain a challenge for these nutty hosts.

"Bring" and "take" are often mistakenly switched. "Bring" shows action *toward* the speaker. "Take" shows action *away from* the speaker. Use the "come, go" analogy. "Bring" is like "come." "Take" is like "go." Instead of, "*Bring* ear plugs to next week's All-State Drummer Competition," say, "*Take* ear plugs." (You're not at the Drummer Competition; you're just reading about it. You will "go" to the competition; you're not there now.)

Right
Take this toilet paper to the outhouse.

Wrong
Bring this toilet paper to the outhouse.

? Why? The person making the request is not in the outhouse at the moment. Use "take."

Usually the error comes in using "bring" for "take." You wouldn't hear, "Please take me some eggs."

If your toaster breaks, **take** (*not* **bring**) it in for service.
(You're not at the toaster repair shop. "Go," *not* "come," to the shop.)

Chelsea **takes** (*not* **brings**) Prissy to see the vet weekly.
(She's not at the vet's now. "Go," *not* "come," to the vet's.)

I'm **taking** (*not* **bringing**) a speech draft to Senator Feinstein.
(You're *not* with her at the moment. "Go," *not* "come," to her office.)

Jeeves will **bring** (*not* **take**) the Jaguar here after the tea.
(Jeeves's action is toward the tea drinkers. Jeeves will "come here," *not* "go there.")

TIP: Ask, "Are you there?" or "Am I there?" If so, use "bring." If not, use "take."

BRITICISMS (BRITISHISMS)

We still use words or phrases borrowed from the British, but in the United States, their meanings, spellings, or usage may have changed. These Briticisms (Brit´ ih siz imz) can be intriguing and give insight into our language.

The **effects** of Sadie's fifteen-bean soup last for hours. (*Not,* **affects**—see page 23.)

Word Meanings

American	British
apartment	flat
cookie	biscuit
elevator	lift
French fries	chips
private boarding school	public school
spool of thread	reel of cotton
subway	underground, tube
thumbtack	drawing pin
truck	lorry
sweater	jumper

Pronunciation

Pronunciation differs, too. Examples:

	American	British
schedule	(sked´ jool)	(shed´ yool)
leisure	(leezh´ er)	(lehzh´ er)

Punctuation

In American English, commas and periods appear inside the quotation (" ." or " ,"); in British English, they appear outside (" ". or " ",). Other British variations: a greater use of hyphens, unspaced ellipses, and the use of single quotes for double quotes and vice versa.

Spelling

The most notorious British spellings are the final *re* and *our* and the doubled *l*. In British English, it's *theatre, humour,* and *cancelled;* in American English, *theater, humor,* and *canceled.* In British English, it's *aeroplane, armour, centre, harbour, honour,* and *traveller;* in American English, the words are spelled *airplane, armor, center, harbor, honor,* and *traveler.*

Another difference is the British use of *c* for *s* and *s* for *c* or *z*, in words like *dramatise* and *licence.* The American words are *dramatize* and *license.*

There are also variations in English in Australia. Some samples:

American	Australian
barbecue grill	barbie
friend	mate
trash can	wheely bin

Her majesty ordered embossed **stationery**. (*Not,* **stationary**—see page 90.)

BULLETS *(See asterisks, page 38.)*

In lists, bullets (•) highlight important points and let readers scan material quickly. Introduce a bulleted list with a colon.

There are different ways to format bullets. Whichever method you choose, be consistent. Don't mix formats within a single list or document.

In this example, each bullet starts with an order, the imperative mood of the verb—"make," "be," and "put":

- Make each point parallel.

- Be concise.

- Put a period at the end of each statement if starting with capitals or if the bulleted items complete a sentence begun above the list.

- Make bulleted lists easier to read, indenting them slightly farther to the right than your paragraph indentation (as shown).

Another approach is to use semicolons at the end of each statement, add "and" before the last item on the list, and end the bulleted list with a period. Some lists with headers have no punctuation marks after bulleted items.

Classic Clothing Labels:

- Gucci

- Celine

- Loewe

- Louis Vuitton

- Ann Taylor

C

CALVARY, CAVALRY

Calvary (Cal´ vuh ree—say the *l*) is a historic site near Jerusalem. The word "cavalry" (cav´ uhl ree) means military troops who ride on horseback or in motorized vehicles. Be careful pronouncing these two.

Kathleen made a pilgrimage to **Calvary.**

Major Poulet called in the **cavalry.**

Things look **bad** on the Fashion Fest runway. (*Not,* **badly**—see page 18.)

CAN, MAY

9 CHICKWEED LANE by Brooke McEldowney

Can? May? There's a difference.

 Right
May I have that last raspberry cream truffle?

 Wrong
Can I have that last raspberry cream truffle?

? **Why?** "May" asks permission and expresses courtesy: "Is it all right with you if I take the last truffle?" (Yes, but Miss Manners would be greatly displeased.) "Can" expresses ability. (Of course it's possible to take a truffle, but that's not what you're asking.)

I **can** throw the discus four hundred feet.

May I take you to the Sting concert?

DID YOU KNOW: When teamed with another verb, "may" also indicates possibility.

Baby Benjamin **may talk** soon.

CAPITALS

Use capital letters:

▶ For the pronoun "I": It is **I**.

▶ To begin a sentence, unquoted or quoted.

 Crimson paint spilled on the white carpet.

 "One could do worse than be a swinger of birches," is the last line of Robert Frost's famous poem "Birches."

"I have to **lie** down," said Dagwood. (*Not,* **lay**—see page 194.)

45

▶ For the first, last, and all other words—except prepositions, articles ("a," "an," "the"), conjunctions, and the "to" of infinitives—of titles of articles, books, journals, magazines, movies, plays, poems, and radio and television shows and series.

> **Article:** "Ford SUV to Challenge Jeep Wrangler" (Note lowercase *t* on "to.")
> **Book:** *No Such Thing as a Bad Day* (Hamilton Jordan)
> **Journal:** *School Library Journal*
> **Magazine:** *In Style* (The preposition "in" is the first word in this title.)
> **Movie:** *Autumn in New York*
> **Play:** *Two Gentlemen of Verona* (William Shakespeare)
> **Poem:** "Genie in a Jar" (Nikki Giovanni)
> **Radio and TV shows and series:** *Prairie Home Companion, Boston Legal*

▶ With proper nouns.

A second grader once told the Grammar Patrol that a proper noun is "a fancy noun that gets a capital." He was exactly right. Proper nouns are specific, not general. Capitalize the first letter of proper nouns.

Proper nouns include:

> ▸ The days of the week, months, and holidays; specific people; or groups, things, buildings, companies, organizations, and schools.

Sunday	August
Valentine's Day	Johnny Mathis
Backstreet Boys	Bolshoi Ballet
Toyota Camry	Hotel Del Coronado
Hollywood Bowl	Pfizer
Amnesty International	Baseball Hall of Fame
DreamWorks	Stanford University
Elton John AIDS Foundation	Andrew Shue's Do Something Foundation

THE BIG E: Sometimes artists break the capitalization rules. The name of singer k. d. lang appears without capitals. Until the mid-30s, poet Edward Estlin Cummings wrote his name as "e e cummings" (no capitals and no periods). Unconventional spelling and punctuation also marked his writing.

Bette plays **better** with decent clubs. (*Not,* **more better**—see page 60.)

▶ Historical events, documents, or government programs.

Gettysburg Address	**Persian Gulf War**
Bicentennial	**Emancipation Proclamation**
Civil Rights Act of 1964	**Medicare**
Social Security Administration	

▶ People's titles.
Capitalize civil, religious, military, and professional titles when they appear right before a person's name. If the title follows the name, don't capitalize the title. If a title appears without the name of a person, do not capitalize it.

- Civil titles

  President Adams
  John Adams, president of the United States
  the president of the United States

- Religious titles
  Capitalization of titles varies among different religions and denominations. Some examples:

  Rabbi Benno Scheinberg, the rabbi
  the Reverend Grayson Clary
  William Tully, rector of St. Bartholomew's

- Military and professional titles

  Chief of Surgery, Dr. Sujan Wong
  Dr. Sujan Wong, chief of Surgery
  General George S. Patton

Some titles, such as "Speaker of the House," are always capitalized, with or without the person's name. Use capitals for titles and nicknames for people whose names appear in popular culture.

Fans once called Britney Spears the "Queen of Teen."

▶ Names of companies and academic departments, even when they appear after a person's title.

Jenni Prisk, president of Prisk Communication
Ron Josephson, professor of Foods and Nutrition

Gryffindor **swept** the Quidditch finals. (*Not,* **sweeped** —see page 202.)

▸ Family names.

> **Aunt Ruth Nelson** (*but* my aunt, Ruth Nelson)
>   **Mother** (*but* her mother, Gertrude Wigginton)
> **Grandfather Hope** (*but* his paternal grandfather, Norman Hope)

▸ Seasons.
Seasons are not capitalized: "summer," "fall," "winter," "spring."

> In the summer, the Dowlers head for Hawaii.

In academic settings, when seasons denote specific semesters, use a capital letter:

> **Fall 2005**   **Summer 2006**

▸ Religions and holy books, holy days, and words for a Supreme Being.

> | | |
> |---|---|
> | Islam | Talmud |
> | Judaism | Bible |
> | Christianity | Koran |
> | Passover | God |
> | Christmas | Buddha |
> | Ramadan | Allah |

▸ Geographic regions.

> | | |
> |---|---|
> | **New England** | **the Pacific Northwest** |
> | **the Far East** | **the South** |

Do not capitalize directions: 50 miles north of Atlanta.

▸ Languages.

> Mona speaks Farsi.

> Instructions for this computer are in Japanese, English, German, and French.

▸ Names of computer programs.

> | | |
> |---|---|
> | **Adobe Acrobat** | **Internet Explorer** |
> | **Flash** | **Microsoft Word** |
> | **PowerPoint** | **Quicken** |

You're camping in Antarctica? (*Not,* **Your**—see page 209.)

▸ Book series and editions.
Capitalize titles of book series and editions. Use lowercase letters for the words "series" and "edition."

> Gary Paulsen's *Culpepper Adventure* series
> large-type *Reader's Digest* edition

DID YOU KNOW? In naming eras or geologic time periods, don't capitalize the word "era," "period," or "times."

> Jurassic era
> medieval times (*but* the Middle Ages)
> Tertiary period

CAREEN, CAREER

"To careen" is "to lurch or swerve; to tip to the side." As a verb, "to career" is "to move at full speed." (As a noun, "career" means "profession.")

> The Ferrari **careened** into the cantaloupe stand.

> Lucky Day **careered** past Born to Win to take first place by a nose.

CASE *(See pronouns, page 147.)*

Nouns and pronouns have "case." They can be **subjective** (in Grammarspeak, "nominative"), **objective**, or **possessive**. "Subjective" nouns and pronouns are used as subjects. "Objective" nouns and pronouns are used as the objects of verbs or prepositions. "Possessive" nouns and pronouns are used to show ownership. The case you use depends on the job the word does in a sentence.

CHOOSE, CHOSE

"Choose" is a present-tense verb meaning "to select or decide." "Chose," meaning "selected" or "decided," is the past tense of "choose." The past participle is "chosen."

> Last week, I **had chosen** fettuccine Alfredo.

> Yesterday, I **chose** a banana split.

> Today, I **choose** carrots.

Deedee and **I** saddled up. (*Not,* **myself**—see page 151.)

CLAUSES *(See also conjunctions, page 61; phrases, page 133; and predicate, page 140.)*

> *If you haven't got anything nice to say about anybody, come sit next to me.*
> —Alice Roosevelt Longworth

Clauses can be independent or dependent. This famous quotation from Teddy Roosevelt's irascible, eldest daughter has both a dependent and an independent clause.

A **clause** is a group of related words with both a subject and a predicate.

Independent Clauses

Independent clauses contain both a subject and a predicate and can stand on their own as complete sentences. No extra words or phrases are needed for readers to understand an independent clause: It forms a complete thought. (In Grammarspeak, independent clauses may be called "main clauses.") Independent clauses make sense, even if they are only two words long.

> **People notice.**
> *(subject) (predicate)*

Here are some longer independent clauses:

> **I can get to work quickly.**
> *(subject)   (predicate)*

> **The wolf howled at the moon.**
> *(subject)   (predicate)*

Independent clauses are often linked with other clauses by conjunctions, such as "because," "since," "for," and "but."

> I celebrated with cheese pizza **because** my cholesterol went down.

Dependent Clauses

Dependent clauses (in Grammarspeak, called "subordinate clauses") contain a subject and a verb, but are not complete sentences. Words in a dependent clause give more information about a main clause. Dependent clauses cannot stand alone. They depend on a main clause to make sense.

Here are some dependent clauses:

when I take BART	**which was shining brightly**
what you wear	**whoever hired Chris Erskine**

Terry plays Boggle with Jeannie and **me**. (*Not,* **I**—see page 149.)

Dependent Clauses as Different Parts of Speech

Dependent clauses do different jobs. When combined with independent clauses, dependent clauses can act as adverbs, adjectives, nouns, or the objects of prepositions.

The independent and dependent clause examples on page 50 can be combined to create sentences like these:

When I take BART, I can get to work quickly.
(dependent clause—adverb)   *(independent clause)*

The wolf howled at the moon, which was shining brightly.
(independent clause)   *(dependent clause—adjective)*

People notice what you wear.
(independent clause) *(dependent clause—noun)*

I tip my hat to whoever hired *L.A. Times* columnist Chris Erskine.
(independent clause)   *(dependent clause—object of preposition)*

Clauses can also be essential (restrictive) or nonessential (nonrestrictive). *(For tips on punctuating these clauses, see that, which, page 154.)*

TIP: Don't confuse dependent clauses with phrases. While dependent clauses do have both a subject and a predicate, phrases don't have both.

CLICHÉS

Clichés are expressions that have been used so often they have become trite:

right as rain	black as night	pretty as a picture
cunning as a fox	bald as a billiard ball	neat as a pin
pearls of wisdom	roll off the tongue	smooth as butter

Avoid clichés **like the plague**! Find fresh ways to describe things.

COLLECTIVE NOUNS *(See nouns, page 118.)*

Collective nouns describe persons or things that act as a single unit. Here are some examples: *assembly, audience, band, class, committee, corps, crew, crowd, faculty, family, flock, group, jury, nation, pair, panel, pod, press, series, set.* A prepositional phrase with a plural object often follows the collective noun.

A **pod of whales** swam past.
(collective noun)(prepositional phrase)

Lee showed us her **mementos** of Africa. (*Not,* **momentos**—see page 113.)

51

Collective nouns usually take singular verbs. To check your verb form, substitute the singular pronoun "it" for the collective noun.

The **faculty votes** tomorrow. (*It* votes.)
(*collective noun*) (*singular verb*)

The **crew dances** a jig. (*It* dances.)
(*collective noun*) (*singular verb*)

The Hughes **family** often **travels**. (*It* travels.)
(*collective noun*) (*singular verb*)

The **flock** of geese **flies** in perfect formation. (*It* flies.)
(*collective noun*)   (*singular verb*)

TIP: Corporations act like collective nouns, even if the company's name is plural. Although a specific company may have many employees, you should refer to it as a single entity.

Merck manufactures a drug to treat osteoporosis. (*It* manufactures.)
(*singular noun*) (*singular verb*)

Brinkley Brothers sells lottery tickets. (*It* sells.)
(*singular noun*)   (*singular verb*)

THE BIG E: Sometimes collective nouns *don't* act as a unit. They take singular or plural verbs, depending on what follows. Use a singular verb if the collective noun is acting together as a group. Use a plural verb if group members act independently as individuals.

Singular:
The **panel voted** to fund the new stadium. (*It* voted.)
(*collective noun*) (*singular verb*)

Plural:
The **panel** of doctors **were** not of one mind.
(*collective noun*)   (*plural verb*)
(Each doctor had a differing opinion. *They* were.)

Singular:
The **couple wants** matching "Born to Be Wild" tattoos. (*It* wants.)
(*collective noun*) (*singular verb*)

Plural:
A **couple** of days **are needed** to distress my new jeans.
(*collective noun*)   (*plural verb*)
(*They* are needed.)

It sounds **as if** Chloë loves singing. (*Not,* **like**—see page 38.)

These collective nouns are the most frequent switch-hitters: *couple, majority, number, percent, press,* and *total.* Let the words that follow collective nouns and the meanings of the sentences help you decide whether the verb is singular or plural.

COLONS

Colons (:) signal that information, an explanation, or a long quotation lies ahead. Put one space after a colon.

> Flash from humorist Dave Barry: "A group of psychology researchers has made the breakthrough discovery that—prepare to be astounded—males and females are different."

Use a colon:

▶ After a business letter greeting.

> Dear Mr. Spielberg:

▶ To introduce a list.

> That year, three names dominated U.S. track and field: Maurice Green, Michael Johnson, and Marion Jones.

> Political campaigns are always the same: flag waving, baby smooching, and lofty speeches. (No capital on "flag.")

▶ Before an explanation.

> Remember this Murphy's Law: Any empty horizontal surface will be piled high within minutes.

▶ With a long quotation.

> *Los Angeles Times* columnist Roy Rivenberg made this observation in his article "The Bumbling Gourmet": "Although I told my panel of reviewers that snarky comments would make this article funnier, they insisted everything was first-rate."

Capitalize the first letter of a full quotation or of any complete sentence that follows a colon.

▶ To show time.

> Madame Solombra reads palms daily from 3:30 to 11:30 P.M.

> Driver interviews at Cam-Mar Growers start at 8:30 A.M.

We **have hardly** any Tootsie Rolls left. (*Not,* **don't have hardly**—see page 117.)

▶ To indicate a subtitle of a book.

Mother Jones: Fierce Fighter for Workers' Rights

Soujourner Truth: A Life, a Symbol

Do not use a colon:

▶ After "such as." (Do put a comma before "such as.")

Courageous leaders, such as Desmond Tutu and Nelson Mandela, guided South Africa's transition from apartheid.
(*Not*, **leaders: such as Desmond Tutu.**)

Include life's necessities, such as belly laughs, naps, and a spicy novel.
(*Not*, **necessities: such as belly laughs.**)

▶ Between a verb and its object.

Rodrigo **danced** the **rumba, fox trot,** and **samba**.
      (*verb*)   (*direct object*)
(*Not*, **danced: the rumba.**)

The three top teams **were Michigan, Penn State,** and **Wisconsin**.
                      (*verb*)   (*object complement*)
(*Not*, **top teams were: Michigan.**)

▶ Between a preposition and its object.

Send petty-cash memos **to Gates, Turner,** and **Trump**.
                       (*preposition*)   (*object of the preposition*)
(*Not*, **to: Gates.**)

COMMAS

A comma (,) signals a pause, as if taking a breath. Put one space after a comma. Use this versatile punctuation mark:

▶ To separate an introductory word or phrase from the rest of the sentence. *(See conjunctions as adverbs, page 64.)*
With introductory phrases, sources differ as to whether or not to use a comma. Some experts say to use a comma after one or two words; others say three or more. Sometimes the comma is needed for clarity.

Moreover, you can't wear knee socks with a rhinestone gown.

Are stocks **more risky** than Blackjack? (*Not*, **more riskier**—see page 60.)

At first, Shanna thought Arturo looked like a Greek god.

After swimming laps, Evelyn took a shower.

As Tippi Hedren's daughter, Melanie Griffith knew the Hollywood scene.

▶ To indicate direct address, when someone is speaking to someone else.

Give me those See's Candies right now, Arthur!

▶ To signal a change of subject or action.

Lady Alona slew the dragon, polished her nails, then took a nap.

▶ To separate two independent clauses joined by a conjunction.

Bernardo loved to eat, and his ample girth showed it.

▶ To separate spoken words from the rest of the sentence.

"The camel ride to the pyramids begins at dawn," our guide told us.

▶ To separate two adjectives that modify the same noun. *(See also compound adjectives, page 14.)*

Ashley Judd has a spirited, friendly personality.

The automated, fast-moving assembly line outpaced the robot.

▶ To separate words that signal that an example is coming.

  ▸ Use a comma before (but not after) "such as" or "like" when a list with commas follows:

    I love Thai food, **such as** pad thai, coconut soup, and spring rolls.

    He feeds the large zoo animals, **like** elephants, rhinos, and hippos.

  ▸ Use a comma before and after "as in," "namely," and "that is."

    Marty knows his food groups, **as in,** chocolate, ice cream, and cookies.

    Two veteran interviewers, **namely,** Tim Russert and Larry King, ranked highly among listeners.

    Use common sense in the wilderness, **that is,** don't take risks.

The Mighty Ducks moved **toward** a winning season. (*Not,* **towards**—see page 188.)

▶ To separate items in a series with serial commas. (*See legal writing, page 107.*)

A serial comma is one used before "and" or "or" in a series of more than two words.

> The Gipsy Kings have roots in France, North Africa, Spain, **and** India.

> Networking Ad: "The Best Way to Motivate, Entice, **or** Schmooze."

Should you use serial commas? Sources differ. The Grammar Patrol likes serial commas for the clarity they provide. Although newspapers and magazines often don't use serial commas, we recommend them in formal writing.

▸ Don't use a comma when the words "and" or "or" separate each item in a series.

> My favorite ice cream flavors are Chocolate Heaven **and** Cherry Garcia **and** Chunky Monkey.

▸ In names of law firms, serial commas are often omitted.

> Bartholomew, Horton & Oobleck

The meaning is clear without the comma.

More Comma Clues

▶ When an independent clause comes first, don't use a comma to separate the independent clause from the dependent clause that follows. (*See clauses, page 50.*)

 Right
Maria went **along because** Arnold was nominated for an Oscar.

Wrong
Maria went **along, because** Arnold was nominated for an Oscar.

? **Why?** Dependent clauses often begin with conjunctions—"because," "unless," "while," and others. In this sentence, the dependent clause "because Arnold was nominated . . ." is needed for the rest of the sentence to make sense. Don't separate it with a comma. If the clauses were reversed, the comma would be needed. The long dependent clause now becomes an introductory clause.

Because Arnold was nominated for an Oscar, Maria went along.

Anna surveyed the building **site**. (*Not,* **cite** or **sight**—see page 88.)

▶ Don't use a comma between a subject and its verb.

Ad: <u>**How you look,**</u> <u>**can depend**</u> on how you look on paper.
       (subject)   *(verb)*
(Delete that comma!)

▶ In American English, a comma never falls outside of quotation marks. The same goes for periods. *(See quotation marks, page 163.)*

COMMA SPLICE *(See incomplete sentences, page 99.)*

COMPARE, CONTRAST *(See compare to, compare with, below.)*

The verb "to compare" looks at likenesses and differences. "To contrast" looks at differences, often noting opposite qualities.

Let's **compare** these two swimsuits.

Eddie's chartreuse tie **contrasts** wildly with his purple shirt.

Students are often asked to "compare and contrast" two things. In fact, the word "compare" alone will do. When you compare one thing with another, you look at both likenesses and differences.

COMPARE TO, COMPARE WITH *(See phrasal verbs, page 131.)*

Use "compare to" to liken dissimilar items. "Compare to" is often figurative.

Frieda **compared** her husband's snoring **to** a Harley at full throttle.

Use "compare with" to show contrast in like items: comparing how two things are both alike and different. "Compare with" is usually literal.

Compared with last month's electric bill, this month's was a disaster.

COMPARISONS *(See also adjectives, page 14, and adverbs, page 17.)*

"Mirror, mirror, on the wall, who's the **fairest** of us all?"

Sorry, Evil Queen—Snow White's the *fairest* in the land. She's *superlative*.
Adjectives and some adverbs not only describe and modify; they can also compare. The degrees of comparison are **positive** (the basic form of the word), **comparative** (two things), and **superlative** (more than two).

King Schnozola is **too** timid for fencing. (*Not,* to—see page 188.)

Positive	Comparative	Superlative
beautiful	more beautiful	most beautiful
easy	easier	easiest
flexible	less flexible	least flexible
warm	warmer	warmest

Comparative Adjectives

▶ Use the comparative form of an adjective to compare two things. To form the comparative, add an **er** ending, or add "more" or "less" to most one-syllable words:

> **young:** younger or more/less young
> **wild:** wilder or more/less wild
> **dense:** denser or more/less dense
> **dark:** darker or more/less dark

> To Zelda, pole vaulting seemed **safer** (or **more safe**) than sky diving.

THE BIG E: Don't add **er** to some one- or two-syllable words, like the informal adjective "fun." Instead of "funner," say, "more fun."

> **more ancient** (*not* "ancienter")
> **more wrinkled** (*not* "wrinkleder")

▶ With two-syllable words ending in **y**, drop the **y** and add **er**, or use "more" or "less" before the word.

> **silly:** sillier, more/less silly   **gaudy:** gaudier, more/less gaudy
> **zany:** zanier, more/less zany   **muddy:** muddier, more/less
> **muddy**

▶ With words of three or more syllables, use "more" or "less" before the word.

> **less bountiful**   **more punctual**   **more intelligent**

▶ You can also modify the comparative form with the adverb "much."

> Pollack's paintings were **much sloppier** than those by Dalí.
> *(comparative)*

THE BIG E: You can use the comparative form with the pronoun "other," even when you mean more than two.

> Cody's bunny suit was **cuter** than the **other** costumes.

Do **Nigel and he** call that broom closet an office? (*Not,* **Nigel and him**—see page 148.)

Superlative Adjectives

▶ Use the superlative form to compare more than two things.

San Francisco is the **least affordable** city in California.

To form the superlative, just add the ending **est** to most one-syllable and some two-syllable words, or add "most" or "least" before some two-syllable words. (Change an ending **y** to **i** if needed.)

fastest	messiest	silliest
most savvy	most sour	least athletic

Anna Kournikova was once the **highest** earner in pro tennis.

▶ With words of three or more syllables, use "most" or "least."

least dangerous	most beautiful	least vulnerable

THE BIG E: You can't add **est** to some words, like the informal adjective "fun." Instead of "funnest," say, "most fun."

Comparisons Using "Old" or "Young"

You need to know how many people or things are involved in order to decide whether to use **er** or **est** after words like "old" or "young."

Camilla is the **younger** of the two sisters. (Two: comparative)

The Rio is the **oldest** of our six cars. (More than two: superlative)

The words "elder" and "eldest" are most often used to compare people, and usually indicate age or seniority. (But these are yielding to "older" and "oldest.")

Our **eldest** son is president of Spin-Around Yo-Yos. (Three other sons also work in the business.)

SHERMAN'S LAGOON by Jim Toomey

Witch Hekkaba had her wart **frozen** off. (*Not,* **froze**—see page 204.)

Irregular Comparatives

Some adjectives are irregular in the comparative and superlative. Just as chameleons change color, irregular comparatives change form.

Positive	Comparative	Superlative
good	better	best
bad	worse	worst

Common Mistakes: Comparative and Superlative

Stay out of double trouble and avoid:

▶ Double comparatives.

 Right
Gambling is **riskier** (or **more risky**) than hang gliding.

 Wrong
Gambling is **more riskier** than hang gliding.

? **Why?** Don't double up in the comparative. Gambling is either "riskier" or "more risky," never "more riskier" than hang gliding. Use *er* or "more," not both.

▶ Double superlatives.

Right
The **most swift** (or **swiftest**) wide receiver of the 1990s was Jerry Rice.

Wrong
The **most swiftest** wide receiver of the 1990s was Jerry Rice.

? **Why?** Don't double up in the superlative. Jerry was either the "most swift" or "the swiftest" wide receiver. Use "most" or *est*, not both.

COMPLEMENT, COMPLIMENT

As a verb, "to complement" means "to supplement" or "to make complete." As a noun, "complement" means "a supplement or a complete set." A complement *completes.*

As a verb, "compliment" expresses praise; as a noun, a "compliment" is a praising remark or an expression of courtesy.

> That polka-dotted scarf **complements** your striped clown outfit.

> Harvey's mom baked a full **complement** of Super Bowl snacks.

> Mr. Dithers **complimented** the class on their dissection of sheep's eyeballs.

Whom shall I call about this silverfish invasion? (*Not,* **who**—see page 155.)

The puppy got lavish **compliments** during Canine Companion training.

TIP: "Complementary" and "complimentary" are also commonly confused. Think of "complementary" as "completing" or "supplying needs or something lacking."

Monet chose **complementary** paint colors.

"Complimentary" means "expressing or resembling a compliment" or "given free as a courtesy or to repay a favor."

The carrot smoothies are **complimentary**.

COMPLEMENTS *(See object complements, page 123, and subject complements, page 184.)*

COMPOUND ADJECTIVES *(See adjectives, page 14.)*

COMPOUND NOUNS *(See nouns, page 118.)*

COMPOUND SENTENCES *(See sentences, page 174.)*

COMPOUND SUBJECTS *(See subject, page 183.)*

CONJUNCTIONS

Imagination is more important than knowledge.

—Albert Einstein

Conjunctions are connectors. *(See the "than" in Albert Einstein's quote.)* Common conjunctions include *after, also, although, and, as, because, but, even though, however, instead, nevertheless, or, otherwise, since, so, than, therefore, though, unless, until, when, while,* and *yet.*

Some conjunctions have specific jobs. On the lists of conjunction types below, note that a conjunction may appear on more than one list.

QVC played a big **role** in her overdrawn account. (*Not,* **roll**—see page 90.)

Coordinating Conjunctions

Coordinating conjunctions connect elements of equal rank: words to words, phrases to phrases, clauses to clauses, or sentences to sentences. The seven coordinating conjunctions are *and, but, for, nor, or, so,* and *yet.*

> lacy shorts **or** silk boxers (word to word)
>   *(conjunction)*

> Buddy Holly's glasses **and** Jim Croce's lyrics (phrase to phrase)
>   *(conjunction)*

> I'll make coffee **so** you won't fall asleep. (clause to clause)
>   *(conjunction)*

> I got rid of my nose ring, **but** I kept my dreads. (sentence to sentence)
>   *(conjunction)*

Tips on Compound Subjects Linked with "Or"

▶ If a compound subject is made up of two singular words joined by "or," use a singular verb.

> **Jocelyn or Vladamir orders** the pizza each Friday. (*She or he* orders.)
> *(compound subject) (singular verb)*

▶ If a compound subject is made up of two plural words joined by "or," use a plural verb.

> **The bats or the vampires** usually **appear** first. (*They* appear.)
> *(compound subject)*   *(plural verb)*

▶ Some compound subjects contain both singular and plural words. The word closest to the verb determines if the verb is singular or plural.

> **The trumpeters or the majorette leads** the parade.
> *(compound subject)*   *(singular verb)*

In this compound subject, the singular noun "majorette" is closest to the verb. Say, "*She* leads."

> **A cackling hyena or squealing boars mimic** your boyfriend's voice.
> *(compound subject)*   *(plural verb)*

In this compound subject, the plural noun "boars" is closest to the verb. Say, "*They* mimic."

Lawrence **graduated from** high school. (*Not,* **graduated** high school page 183.)

Conjunction Pairs

Two conjunctions often work together in the same sentence to make a point. The sentence parts these conjunctions introduce must be parallel (of equal weight). Position the conjunctions close to what they compare. (In Grammarspeak, conjunction pairs are called "correlative conjunctions.")

Common Conjunction Pairs

although, nevertheless	although, yet	both, and
either, or	if, then	neither, nor
not only, but also	when, then	whether, or
whether, or not	where, there	

Neither George **nor** Gracie sails. **Neither** Gracie **nor** her cats swim. (The word closest to the verb determines if it's singular or plural. *She* sails: singular verb. *They* swim: plural verb.)

If you love children, **then** teaching is for you.

The wave took **not only** my snorkel mask, **but also** my suit.

As, As and So, As

The conjunction pair "as, as" is usually *positive*.

Jill is **as** fond of chocolate **as** Donna is.

The pair "so, as" is usually *negative*.

The stock market was not **so** volatile today **as** it was yesterday.

Subordinating Conjunctions

Subordinating conjunctions connect parts of a sentence (clauses or phrases) that are not of equal rank. Subordinating conjunctions include *because, if, since, until, when, where,* and *while.* They often link a dependent clause to an independent clause.

Because the monster lurks beneath, I'm afraid of Loch Ness.

Here, the conjunction "because" forms a dependent clause ("Because the monster lurks beneath") connected to an independent clause ("I'm afraid of Loch Ness").

We can't see the stars **until** after sundown.

Here, the conjunction "until" links a prepositional phrase ("after sundown") to the independent clause ("We can't see the stars").

If I **were** you, I wouldn't wear stretch pants. (*Not,* **was**—see page 197.)

Conjunctions as Adverbs

Some conjunctions do two jobs at once. (In Grammarspeak, these are called "conjunctive adverbs.") They may connect sentence parts, acting as conjunctions. At the same time, they modify other words, acting as adverbs.

Conjunctive adverbs include *consequently, however, meanwhile, moreover, nevertheless, similarly, still, then,* and *thus.* You'll often find them at the beginning of a sentence or a clause. A comma usually follows these adverbs.

The pool was freezing; **still,** I needed to swim.
(conjunctive adverb)

Weeks of uncertainty followed the election. **Finally,** it was over.
(conjunctive adverb)

TIP: Don't switch the conjunction "than" with the adverb "then." Use "than" to compare. Use "then" to show time.

Santa's chunkier **than** the Pillsbury Doughboy.

We ate, **then** ran.

CONSONANTS, VOWELS

ZITS by Jerry Scott and Jim Borgman

Consonants are all the letters of the alphabet except the vowels—*a, e, i, o, u,* and sometimes *y.* With the names "Yvonne" and "Yvette," for instance, you hear a vowel sound—"Ee von," "Ee vet." In words like "mystify," "plenty," "pigmy," and "try," the *y* also makes a vowel sound.

CONTRACTIONS *(See apostrophes, page 30, and verbs, page 190.)*

CURLY QUOTES *(See quotation marks, page 163.)*

Charlene **has** to practice her violin now. (*Not,* **have, gots,** or **gotta**—see page 84.)

D

DANGLING PARTICIPIAL PHRASES *(See also verbs, page 201.)*

Dangle? Isn't that what earrings do? Or bungee jumpers? And what *is* a participle anyway? With regular verbs, a participle is the verb form that ends in *ing* in the present tense and *d, ed,* or *t* in the past tense.

tearing	chuckling	waxing
snored	kicked	dreamt

▶ Combine participles with other words to make a participial phrase.

waxing the surfboard
tearing her hair out
kicked through the goal posts

▶ Position participial phrases close to the word or words they modify. Be sure that a participial phrase at the beginning of a sentence refers to the subject.

<u>Waxing his surfboard</u>, Rob Machado eyed the waves.

<u>Tearing her hair out</u>, Bipsy dissolved into tears.

<u>Kicked through the goalposts</u>, the **football** sailed into the stands.

▶ Make clear what word or words the participial phrase modifies. Otherwise—oh horrors—your participial phrase dangles! The results can be downright funny.

<u>Chasing Jesse James</u>, the **locomotive** carrying Detective Pinkerton chugged down the track. (Go, locomotive, go!)

<u>For drawing on the wall</u>, **Grandmother** grounded Freddy. (Is Grandmother the wall artist?)

Tanner faced the interviewers, his **shoes** polished and <u>wearing his only suit</u>. (Are his shoes wearing the suit?)

▶ Rearrange or reword to fix a dangling phrase. Banish dangling participles by rearranging or rewording sentences or by adding a connecting conjunction.

Divide the wild rice between **Kay and me.** (*Not,* **Kay and I**—see page 149.)

65

Dangler:
Wearing a black negligee, he noticed her. (Ooo-la-la!)

The Fix:
Wearing a black negligee, she drew his attention.

Dangler:
Nestled between Providence and Fall River, Ned saw the fishing boats. (Hope the water was warm!)

The Fix:
Ned saw the fishing **boats** **nestled between Providence and Fall River**.

Dangler:
Blessed with superior stamina, Marie's **sneakers** pounded the pavement. (Sneakers in training?)

The Fix:
Blessed with superior stamina, Marie ran. Her sneaker-clad feet pounded the pavement.

DID YOU KNOW? Certain present participles introduce an idea, but stand apart from the rest of the sentence. The most common examples are "regarding," "concerning," and "according to."

> **Considering** how much the man hated him, Harry Potter couldn't believe that Snape had come through.

TIP: Avoid starting sentences with "being as" or "being that." It's awkward and wordy. Use "because" or "since" instead.

> "**Since** it was raining, I stayed home." (*Not,* "**Being as** it was raining . . .")

DASHES (*See also hyphens, page 91, and quotation marks, page 163.*)
Dashes are informal. They set off single words, phrases, or clauses to emphasize, draw attention, or add information. They come in two sizes. Em dashes (—) are long dashes. En dashes (–) are half as long, but longer than a hyphen. Use an em dash with words. Use an en dash with numbers (think "n" for "number").

A massage never hurt **anybody.** (*Not,* **nobody**—see page 116.)

You can use dashes alone or in pairs. No space comes before or after a dash.

> Trina always bought her Jaguars online—so much less bother, she said.

> Hedley's auburn curls—thanks to Loving Color No. 82—gleamed in the sun.

Em Dashes

Use em dashes:

▶ To show a sudden break or abrupt change.

> "I'll be okay, really—wait, what's that noise?" The phone dropped.

▶ To show a side comment.

> "Familiarity breeds contempt—and children," Mark Twain once said.

▶ To explain or add information.

> In *Number the Stars,* Lois Lowry wrote, "Surely that gift—the gift of human decency—is the one that all countries hunger for still."

▶ To show hesitation or stammering.

> "I can't believe—" Clara gasped.

> "That's m——m——my blankie," stammered Dylan.

▶ To show attributions.

> *We may have a winner here!*
> —George Aldrich, Rotten Sneaker Contest judge

En Dashes

Use en dashes:

▶ With math problems. (Use spaces when the en dash is a subtraction sign.)

> $17 - 9 - 8$

▶ With sets of dates or times.

> **January 6–February 3**   WWII, 1941–45   8:30 A.M.–10:30 P.M.

▶ With ranges of numbers.

> Futon Sale: Just $49.99–$99.99

Peter did **well** in marketing. (*Not,* **good**—see page 19.)

Dandelion Wine, pages 53–54

▶ To indicate birth years for living persons.

Bindi Sue Irwin (1998–), daughter of Steve Irwin, crocodile hunter.

▶ To link two-word modifiers and sets of letters.

They crossed the New York–New Jersey border at midnight.

San Diego–Maui flight

FDR–JFK link

Forming Dashes

With a typewriter, make an em dash with two unspaced hyphens and an en dash with one. With a computer, check your software manual to learn how to form the em and en dash in your word processing program.

DID YOU KNOW? Dashes are sometimes incorrectly called "slashes." (*See slashes, page 176.*)

DATA, DATUM (*See Latin plurals, page 106.*)

DATES (*See numbers, page 120.*)

When a full date, not just a year, is used in a sentence, follow it with a comma.

On **March 4, 1995,** Rex Morgan finally proposed to June, his comic strip love.

When listing only the month and year (not a specific day), skip the comma.

The North Woods adventure of **July 2001** (*not* July, 2001) included great fishing, a tornado, fabulous food, and a canoe tipover. (This is preferable to writing "July **of** 2001.")

Here's a quick review of Math 101:

▶ Cardinal numbers tell how many: 1, 2, 3; one, two, three . . .

▶ Ordinal numbers indicate order: 1st, 2nd, 3rd; first, second, third . . .

When a date appears after a month, use cardinal numbers. Don't add *st, nd, rd,* or *th.*

Bill and **she** are going to Stratford. (*Not,* **her**—see page 148.)

The wedding was August **12**, 2000. (*Not,* August 12**th**, 2000.)
or
The wedding was on August **12**. (*Not,* August 12**th**.)

Only use an ordinal number when you leave out the month.

Their wedding was the **12th**.

Chocolat is due back by the **19th**.

More rarely, spell out an ordinal number if it appears before the month.

RSVP by the **second** of December.

No commas are needed when the date comes before the month, as it often appears in academic or military writing.

7 December 1941

The *Kitty Hawk* departs **5** January 2003.

DECLARATIVE MOOD *(See sentences, page 174, and verbs, page 197.)*

DEFUSE, DIFFUSE

The verb "defuse" (dee fyooz´) means "to make less dangerous, tense, embarrassing, or hostile."

The judge for the Best Breeder contest **defused** herd tension by crowning two Holsteins, Gert and Olive, as blue ribbon winners.

As a verb, "diffuse" (dih fyooz´) means "to disperse, spread out, or scatter."

Wind **diffused** the dandelion puffs.

As an adjective, "diffuse" (dih fyoose´—rhymes with "moose") means "dispersed or widely scattered."

Diffuse constellations dot the night sky.

DESERT, DESSERT

As a noun, "desert" (deh´ zert) means "a dry, sandy region." As a verb, "desert" (dih zert´) means "to abandon." A "dessert" (deh zert´) is the last course of a meal. (Remember the double **s** by thinking "strawberry **s**hortcake.")

Edgie led his Young Life group on a hike in the Anza-Borrego **Desert**.

Members of the research team **attempt** cloning ants. (*Not,* **attempts**—see page 26.)

Crock **deserted** his post.

For **dessert**, Pat served her famous lemon meringue pie.

DID YOU KNOW? "Desert"—when pronounced "deh zert´"—also means a deserved reward or punishment. In the phrase "they got their **just deserts**," the word "deserts" is correctly spelled with one *s*.

DIAGRAMMING SENTENCES

Building a house is much like fitting words together. A blueprint guides the construction of the house. Similarly, a diagram of a sentence creates a blueprint for sentence structure.

A century ago, almost every schoolchild knew how to diagram, or "parse," a sentence. Students broke sentences into parts—to figure out the form and function of each word and how the parts were related.

The Grammar Patrol confesses that we loved diagramming sentences in school. But today, many people find diagramming old-fashioned and unnecessary.

With diagramming, the controversy comes with more complex English sentences. They are difficult to diagram and make you focus on individual words and their jobs instead of how words work together to create meaning. There are also several different ways to diagram sentences.

Nevertheless, it's handy to know how diagramming works. Here are some samples of one way to diagram simple sentences:

▶ John loves words.

subject	*predicate*
John	**loves words**
(*noun*)	(*verb*) (*direct object*)

Sarah reads voraciously.

subject	*predicate*
Sarah	**reads**
(*noun*)	(*verb*) *voraciously* (*adverb*)

Nikki rowed really **well**. (*Not,* **good**—see page 19.)

▶ Linden especially loves insects.

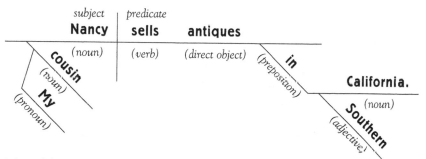

More complex sentences:

▶ My cousin Nancy sells antiques in Southern California.

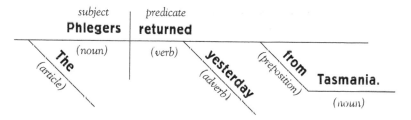

▶ The Phlegers returned yesterday from Tasmania.

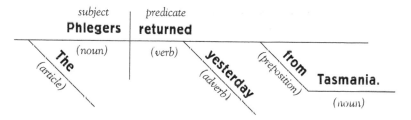

DICTIONARIES

For just when ideas fail, a word comes in to save the situation.

—Johann Wolfgang von Goethe

Dictionaries vary widely in both quality and quantity of entries. It's imperative to have a high-quality current dictionary on hand, such as *Merriam-Webster's Collegiate Dictionary,* Tenth Edition (1994), *The Random House Webster's College Dictionary* (1999), *Webster's New World Dictionary,* Third College Edition (1988, 1997), or *The American Heritage Dictionary,* Third Edition (1992, 1996).

You **have** a problem with my sardine soufflé? (*Not,* **got**—see page 84.)

You can now find many dictionaries on the Internet, such as Merriam-Webster's site, m-w.com, or OneLook Dictionaries' site, www.onelook.com.

DIFFERENT FROM, DIFFERENT THAN (See also clauses, page 50.)

Things differ *from* one another, not *than* one another. Use "different from" to compare—it's almost always the right choice.

Her taste in shoes is **different from** mine.

TIP: Only use "different than" when a clause follows it.

Keiko Matsui's jazz is **different than the jazz Louis Armstrong played**.

(clause)

DISBURSE, DISPERSE

"To disburse" is "to pay out (often money)." "To disperse" means "to move in different directions" or "to make disappear."

The comptroller **disbursed** the lottery bonanza.

The crowd **dispersed** after the appearance of the Accordion Marching Band.

DISINTERESTED, UNINTERESTED

"Disinterested" means "unbiased, neutral." "Uninterested" means "indifferent, not interested."

The boomerang contest called for **disinterested,** agile judges.

Vinnie was **uninterested** in football.

DOUBLE NEGATIVES (See negatives, page 115.)

E

EACH OTHER, ONE ANOTHER

Use the phrase "each other" when talking about two people.

Cleopatra and Marc Antony loved **each other**.

Anne **should have gone** to Bali. (*Not*, **should have went**—see page 204.)

Use the phrase "one another" when talking about more than two people.

The players rooted for **one another** in the game.

EASY MIX-UPS

JEFF MACNELLY'S SHOE by Chris Cassatt and Gary Brooking

While a spell checker would flag "Murry Christmas," it can't help when you choose a word that's spelled right, but isn't the correct word.

Some word pairs, often close in spelling, are easily switched by mistake. A current dictionary can help you avoid such bloopers.

We thank the Blotsons for this Sunday's **alter** flowers. (Should be **altar**.)

Are you confused about "affect," "effect"? "Affluent," "effluent"? Check the alphabetical listings in this book for common word mix-ups.

ELLIPSES

Ellipses are three spaced periods (. . .) that indicate that words or information has been left out.

In using ellipses, your job is to keep the original meaning when you shorten the quote. Sometimes, ad writers intentionally leave out words they don't like, especially when quoting from reviews.

Original Review: I desperately wish I could give this film rave reviews!

Revised Ad Copy: . . . rave reviews!

Use ellipses:

▶ To replace omitted material.

Thor **couldn't** care less about Drusilda's hairdo. (*Not,* **could**—see page 117.)

Original Version: "Soon the classroom was full of girls with their shamisens, spaced out as neatly as chocolates in a box." (*Memoirs of a Geisha*, Arthur Golden)

Shortened Version: The girls were " . . . spaced out as neatly as chocolates in a box."

▶ To indicate pauses, hesitation, or words trailing off:

"No, Alice, I'm . . .," the Cheshire Cat yawned.

Tips on Spacing and Punctuation with Ellipsis Points

▶ Three dots show an omission in a sentence. Put a space before and after the ellipsis points.

Carl Sandburg wrote of Abraham Lincoln, "The more fully Lincoln's varied career is traced . . . the more his genius grows and passes beyond each interpretation."

▶ If the end of a sentence marks the beginning of the omission, use the period, then add the ellipses, for a total of four dots.

E. B. White wrote in *Charlotte's Web*, "Wilbur never forgot Charlotte. . . . It is not often that someone comes along who is a true friend and a good writer. Charlotte was both."

▶ If the ellipses appear at the end of a quotation, put any needed parenthesis, comma, or quotation mark right after the final dot.

Snoopy's stories always begin: "It was a dark and stormy . . ."

▶ If the ellipses show that part of a quoted question is missing, put no space between the ellipses and the question mark.

"How doth the little busy bee . . .?" begins Lizzie's favorite poem.

▶ In a math sequence, put a comma before the ellipses.

5, 10, 15, 20, 25, 30, . . .

▶ In a math series, do not put a comma before the ellipses.

1+ 2 + 4 + 8 + . . .

Other Ellipsis-Point Tips

▶ Don't begin an indented quoted passage with ellipses.

Katie felt **bad** about her house's tilting walls. (*Not,* **badly**—see page 18.)

▶ When you list items in a sentence, don't put a comma before ellipses.

At the convention, you will need hats, balloons, placards, buttons, Advil . . . (*Not,* Advil*, . . .*)

EM AND EN DASHES (*See dashes, page 66.*)

EMAIL

This computer word, which stands for "electronic mail," has entered our lives so quickly that even the experts can't agree how to spell it: "E-mail," "e-mail," or "email." The trend has been toward hitting the fewest number of keys, so "email" is winning.

The word "email" began life as a noun ("I'll check my **emails**"). It has since been "verbed" ("please **email** that draft to me").

Give this fast, efficient communication mode the same attention you would a letter or a phone call, particularly in business settings. Proofread emails carefully and use your spell checker. Remember, you're sending an image of yourself.

SINGLE SLICES by Peter Kohlsaat

My boyfriend loves to write me long romantic emails.

He calls it e-moting.

© 2000 Los Angeles Times Syndicate

More Email Tips

▶ Avoid overusing abbreviations, eliminating punctuation and capitalization, or writing in all capital letters. THAT'S LIKE SHOUTING! Be clear and concise.

▶ Email only messages that you wouldn't mind seeing as headlines in the *New York Times.*

▶ If you forward anecdotes and jokes, delete the cluster of addresses at the top.

EMIGRANT, IMMIGRANT

An "emigrant" is one who leaves a country. An "immigrant" is one who enters a country. The verb forms work the same way. "To emigrate" is "to leave a country." "To immigrate" is "to enter a country."

Nina loves my baked **Alaska.** (*Not,* **elastic**—see page 111.)

The **emigrant** fled Bosnia for political reasons.

Chinese **immigrants** helped build the Transcontinental Railroad.

EMINENT, IMMINENT

The adjective "eminent" means "distinguished, lofty." "Imminent" means "very near, very certain," as in "imminent death."

Doctor Stuart Patton is an **eminent** food scientist.

An attack of "cashew craving" is **imminent.**

ENERVATE, ENERGIZE

Don't confuse these two words. They're opposites. The verb "enervate" means "to weaken, to deprive of energy." "Energize" means "to make energetic."

Katie Couric has an **energizing** presence. (*Not,* **enervating**!)

ENTRÉE, ENTRY

The noun "entrée" means "main course" or "liberty to enter." The noun "entry" means "entrance" or "item on a list."

Eloise relished her **entrée** of eggplant Parmesan.

Margaret's donations to the NAACP gave her **entrée** to the Image Awards.

A telling **entry** on Max's Home Depot list was rat poison.

EPONYMS (*See malapropisms, page 111.*)

Eponyms are words taken from the names of famous people who are known for a certain trait or way of behaving.

That boy will grow up to be an **Einstein.**

The word "malapropism," for instance, comes from Mrs. Malaprop, a play character known for her twists on word choices. Roquefort cheese, with a capital *r,* takes its eponymous name from the Roquefort area of France. The leotard was invented by aerialist Jules Léotard of France, who needed those close-fitting garments for free movement and safety in his high-flying work.

Ron **saw** the Boundary Waters in Minnesota. (*Not,* **seen**—see page 204.)

Other familiar eponymous words:

> diesel engine (Rudolf Diesel)
> mason jar (John Mason)
> Jeeves (for writer P. G. Wodehouse's legendary manservant)
> Mona Lisa smile (for Leonardo da Vinci's enigmatic portrait)

EUPHEMISMS

Euphemisms are mild, vague, or indirect words or phrases substituted for ones that might be considered too harsh or blunt.

> I wept at the news that Steve Allen had **passed away**. (For "died.")

EVERY DAY, EVERYDAY

"Every day" means "each day." The adjective "everyday" means "ordinary, usual."

> **Every day** we have an **everyday** meal: meatloaf.

EXERT, EXPEND

The verb "to exert" means "to use energetically, put forth, put into action." "Expend" means "to spend, use up."

> The protesters **exerted** pressure on the board.

> Jennie **expended** every ounce of energy in the Ironman Triathlon.

EXCLAMATION POINTS

Exclamation points exclaim! They draw attention, emphasize, and demand.

> "Rats!" said Buck, opening the FedEx package. "I ordered teddy bear boxers."

> "Welcome to my home page! I kiss you!" read Mahir Cagri's home page.

Do not use a period or comma after an exclamation point. Use only one exclamation point, not more!!!!! Avoid using exclamation points in formal writing, and use them sparingly in informal writing.

Hand over the **anchovies, George**. (*Not,* **anchovies George**—see page 55.)

EXPLICIT, IMPLICIT

The adjective "explicit" means "stated outright." "Implicit" means "unsaid, understood, implied."

> The recipe gave **explicit** directions for baking chocolate puffs.

> Jared's disapproval was **implicit** in his deep scowl.

F

FARTHER, FURTHER

The adverb "farther" means at a greater distance. (TIP: There's a "far" in "**far**ther.") The adverb "further" means "more distant in degree or time."

> She threw the javelin **farther** than ever before. (This indicates a greater distance.)

> "Look **further**," the soothsayer advised. "A handsome amphibian awaits you." (A Frog Prince is in the wings.)

FERMENT, FOMENT

"To ferment" (fer ment´) is "to undergo a chemical reaction." "To foment" (foh ment´) is "to stir up, to provoke."

> Some fine wines **ferment** in oak casks.

> An unhappy sailor **fomented** a mutiny aboard the ship.

FEWER, LESS (See amount, number, page 28.)

Some grocery stores are replacing their "Ten Items or Less" signs with the correct "Ten Items or Fewer."

"Fewer" answers "how many?" Use "fewer" for things you can count.

fewer home runs	fewer political gaffes
fewer orchids	fewer fruitcakes

"Less" answers "how much?" Use "less" for things you can't count.

less courage	less sickness
less cheating	less laughter

Here's a camping idea for Robin and **them**. (*Not,* **they**—see page 149.)

The exception is the use of "less" with time: Sylvie had **less** than three hours until her Broadway debut.

TIP: Say, "two fewer," but "one less."

FIGURES OF SPEECH *(See literal, literally, page 111; metaphors, page 113; and similes, page 176.)*

CALVIN AND HOBBES by Bill Watterson

"Shall I compare thee to a summer's day?" asks a Shakespearean sonnet. Figures of speech, also known as figurative language, help make creative comparisons. The items compared may be wildly dissimilar, but the reader gets the point. The most common figures of speech are metaphors and similes. Others include hyperbole and puns.

Metaphors
A **metaphor** compares one thing to another, making the comparison appear to be true. (Metaphors don't use "like" or "as.")

> When it comes to girlfriends, Fergus is a fox.

> Brunhilde was a storm cloud when angry.

Similes
A **simile** compares one thing to another, using the prepositions "like" or "as."

> Bronco towered, like Goliath. (Despite his size, Bronco isn't Goliath.)

> Heather is bright as the sun. (Heather is not the sun!)

Hyperbole (Say, "hie per´ buh lee," *not* "hie´ per bowl.")
Hyperbole is deliberate exaggeration used for emphasis or effect.

The people in the courtroom **await** the jury's verdict. (*Not,* **awaits**—see page 26.)

Francesca looks fifty years younger than she is. (Bless that wrinkle cream.)

Al had waited centuries for this moment. (Just call him Methuselah.)

Puns

Kid: "I need some puns."

Alice: "Do you want ballpoint puns or fountain puns?"

Puns are plays on words. A pun compares two dissimilar things by using one word or phrase. Sometimes, the joke includes words that sound alike and so apply two meanings of a single word.

Did you hear about the elf who didn't want to work for Santa anymore, so he set himself up as an independent Clause?

Q. What did Balboa say when he discovered Panama?

A. Isthmus be the place.

Homophones (sound-alike words) provide great material for puns, jokes, and plays on words. (*See homophones, page 87.*)

Sign on a gas station's tow truck: "We Keep You on Our Tows."

FILLERS (*See as, like, page 37, and spoken errors, page 181.*)

In conversation, the word "like" has become an all-purpose part of speech. Overuse of "like" as a filler is ubiquitous.

"Dad, I, **like**, need a new car. Yours is, **like**, totally rusty and, **like**, it's, **like**, torture to drive."

That's too many "likes" for anyone's liking.

An English professor at a prominent East Coast college launched a campaign to abolish the word "like" from students' speech after counting 87 "likes" in an overheard conversation between students. Many schools include speech (minus fillers!) in their graduation requirements.

Occasional fillers can be overlooked. But overusing them in business, educational, or professional situations can distract your listeners and harm your image. The biggest danger is having fillers become so much a part of your speech that you're completely unaware that you use them.

Anyway, where was I? (*Not*, **Anyways**—see page 30.)

DID YOU KNOW? Adding the fillers "honestly" or "to be honest with you" implies that other things you say are not honest.

Quite honestly, this car's a bargain.

IN THE BLEACHERS by Steve Moore

Common Fillers

like	um, uh
totally	actually
basically	clearly
really	honestly, truly
I mean	you know
You know what I mean?	You get (*or* know *or* see) what
Get it?	I'm saying?
See?	No problem.
Whatever.	He/She goes . . .
so (as in, "That is *so* not cool.")	Anyway . . .

The **number** of female senators increased. (*Not,* **amount**—see page 28.)

Tips for Being a Filler-Killer

▶ Be alert: Listen carefully for fillers in spoken language.

▶ Tally: Have a friend track the fillers you use in an hour.

▶ Tape yourself: Record your speech or a presentation, then replay, listening for fillers. Be prepared for a shock.

DID YOU KNOW? Some speaking organizations charge members a fee (from a quarter to $5) for every filler—er, um, uh—used in a speech.

NON SEQUITUR by Wiley

FLOUNDER, FOUNDER

The verb "to flounder" means "to struggle falteringly." (As a noun, a flounder is a flatfish.) "To founder" is "to sink, to fail utterly." (As a noun, "founder" means "one who founds or establishes.")

Confused by twists and turns in the path, the hikers **floundered**.

Lacking good leadership, the desalination project **foundered**.

Thomas Jefferson was a **founder** of the country.

FORMER, LATTER

"Former" means "the first of two listed." "Latter" means "the second of two listed."

We have cashews and corn curls—would you like the **former** (meaning cashews) or the **latter** (meaning corn curls)?

I preferred my **former** clunker to this gas-guzzling SUV.

Your bib overalls or your velvet suit? I'd choose the **latter** for the Oscars.

Edith's **daughters-in-law** are terrific. (*Not*, **daughter-in-laws**—see page 136.)

Don't use "former" or "latter" when talking about more than two items. Use "first, second, third, . . . last."

TIP: Don't confuse "latter" (two *t*'s—the second of two things listed) with "later" (one *t*—the opposite of "earlier").

G

GANTLET, GAUNTLET

The nouns "gantlet" and "gauntlet" are confused so often that their meanings are blurring. For "gantlet," think "ordeal" or "course": "Run the gantlet." For "gauntlet," think of a glove: "Throw down the gauntlet."

MNEMONIC (MEMORY AID): Imagine a **gaunt** person wearing a glove, a **gauntlet**.

GENDER-INCLUSIVE LANGUAGE

He, she, or he/she? Which pronoun is best? Life was so simple before the revolution. Today, it makes sense to be gender inclusive and politically correct. The problem has to do with the third person singular form of the pronoun.

Each angler must clean **his** own fish. (What about the female anglers?)

Many of the solutions for this problem are awkward: he/she, his/her, s/he, or alternating the pronouns "he" and "she." The Grammar Patrol hopes that in the future, some clever grammarian will come up with a great unisex singular pronoun. Until then, consider these strategies for reducing gender bias:

► Use plural nouns and pronouns.

All **firefighters** must care for **their** own equipment.

► Replace the pronoun with an article.

Each student must submit **his** application by November 30.
becomes
Each student must submit **an** application by November 30.

He **sits** in the bathtub during *The Truman Show*. (*Not,* **sets**—see page 195.)

83

▶ Remove the pronouns. (The sentences become shorter, too.)

> An effective leader delegates **his** responsibilities.
>
> *becomes*
>
> An effective leader delegates responsibilities.

▶ Use generic nouns for occupations: mail carrier (for postman), flight attendant (for stewardess), police officer (for policeman), spokesperson (for spokesman), workers (for workman), layperson (for layman), homemaker (for housewife), supervisor (for foreman), news anchor (for anchorman).

▶ Find substitutes for words containing "man." "Man-made" becomes "synthetic." "Man" or "mankind" becomes "human" or "humankind." "Chairman" becomes "chair." "Manpower" becomes "staff."

▶ Avoid suffixes that make a noun feminine when added to words, such as **ess, ette, ix,** and **ienne**. "Actr**ess**" and "comedi**enne**" become "actor" and "comedian."

▶ In business, use titles that don't perpetuate gender stereotypes or marital status: Mr., Ms., Dr.

> Ms. Donna Agins plots her novels in great detail.
>
> Mr. Robert Jones was chief engineer on the submarine project.
>
> Dr. Steven L. Weber is president of San Diego State University.
>
> Dr. Edward Nelson performed the liver transplant.

TIP: If possible, ask people how they wish to be addressed. It might be "Ruth Overheu," "Ms. Ruth Kay Overheu," or "Mrs. Gerald Overheu."

GERUND *(See verbs, page 191.)*

GOT, HAVE

You got [sic] to be careful if you don't know where you're going, because you might not get there.
—Yogi Berra

The verbs "got" and "have" are often confused. "Got" is the past tense of the verb "to get." "Have" is the present tense of the verb "to have."

Cooperation has replaced the "space race." (*Not,* "race". —see page 165.)

Tips for Using "Got" and "Have"

▶ Don't use "got" in the present tense when you mean "have."

Peter, I **have** a great idea for you. (*Not*, I **got**.)

I **have** to go to the Detroit Pistons game later today. (*Not*, I **got to** *or* **gotta**.)

▶ "Got" and "gotten" can both be correct.
Part of the confusion about "got" comes from the past participle. In American English "have gotten" is more common. In British English, "have got" is more common.

Present	Past	Past Perfect
I get	I got	I have gotten *or*
		I have got

Consult the dictionary—you'll find almost a full page of definitions for the verb "get." Shades of meaning separate "I'll get him for this," and "I'll get pizza."

Tips for Using "Got" and "Gotten" with Helping Verbs

▶ American English offers a subtle difference in meaning between "got" and "gotten" when used with helping verbs.

Monica Seles **has got** hundreds of tennis racquets.

Here, "has got" means Monica has the racquets in her possession.

Disney **has gotten** strong reviews for its children's programming.

Here, "has gotten" means Disney has received or acquired the reviews.

SIX CHIX by Kathryn Lemieux

Is that **true**? (*Or*, Is that a **fact**?) (*Not*, **a true fact**—see page 169.)

▶ Don't count on ads to help you with the got-have conundrum. Catchy advertising slogans such as "Got milk?" (or, in Hawaii, "Got poi?") sell products, but reinforce a common error. What the slogans really mean is: "Hey! Do you have any milk?" or "Have you got any milk?" (What makes this confusing is that "have" can be either a verb or a helping verb. In the first example, the verb "have" needs no helping verb; in the second example, the verb "got" does need a helping verb, "have.")

▶ Another common spoken error is taking shortcuts like "gonna" or "gotta" for "going to" or "have to."

> "Jay Leno's **gonna** love this latest scandal." (is going to)

> "Anne's **gotta** visit the Florida Keys." (has got to)

TIP: A related shortcut is the one taken with verbs like "would have," "should have," and "could have." Informally, these often become "woulda," "shoulda," and "coulda." Avoid this.

HANGED, HUNG
Both words are the past tense of the verb "to hang." Use "hanged" when referring to hanging a person: execution by being suspended (the person was hanged until dead). Use "hung" when referring to things you can hang up, such as clothes, doors, pictures.

> The Confederate Army **hanged** Union spy Timothy Webster.

> Hilary **hung** her sequined majorette uniform back in the closet.

HEALTHY, HEALTHFUL
Although the lines are blurring, we recommend using "healthy" when you mean "in good health," and "healthful" when you mean "good for you."

> I stay **healthy** by riding my unicycle.

> Weight Watchers teaches **healthful** eating habits.

Abby, a gorgeous calico cat, **lets** me pet her. (*Not*, let's—see page 109.)

HISTORIC, HISTORICAL *(See articles, page 35.)*

Think of "historic" as "famous in history" or "important in history." Think of "historical" as "based on events of the past." Both words are adjectives; pronounce the *h*. Say, "a historic, a historical" *not* "an 'istoric, an 'istorical."

> Martin Luther King, Jr.'s "I Have a Dream" speech was a **historic** civil rights event.

> Diane Gabaldon's books are based on extensive **historical** research.

HOME, HONE

As a verb, "home" means "to move toward home, a goal, or a target." The verb "hone" means "to sharpen or perfect."

> The exterminator **homed** in on the termites in the wood paneling.

> Don **honed** his carpentry skills while making a coffee table.

HOMOGRAPHS, HOMONYMS, HOMOPHONES *(See its, it's, page 105; their, there, they're, page 187; your, you're, page 209.)*

ZITS by Jerry Scott and Jim Borgman

The term "homonyms" used to cover all words that look or sound alike.

Today "homonym" has been divided into the subsets "homophone" and "homograph." Homophones ("same sound") sound alike, but have different meanings and spellings: one/won, hair/hare. Homographs ("written the same") have the same spelling, but different sounds: "wound," as in, "injury," and "wound," as in, "wrapped."

Fewer than five boys fell asleep during Muggles studies. (*Not,* **less**—see page 78.)

Homophone errors are easy to make.

"Have your dog **spade**." (Make this **spayed**.)

"See you this **Forth** of July!" (Make this **Fourth**.)

"I'm **dyeing** to **meat** you." (Make this **dying** and **meet**.)

No computer spell checker will catch such errors.

Here's a sampling of frequently confused homophones:

aid (v., to help; n., help, something that helps)
aide (n., a helper)

air (n., the gas we breathe)
heir (n., one who will inherit)

bare (adj., not covered, naked)
bear (v., to hold up, support; n., large furry predator)

boarder (n., lodger)
border (n., boundary, edge)

bread (n., food made of baked dough)
bred (v., past tense of "breed")

capital (n., seat of government, wealth)
Capitol (n., government building)

cite (v., to quote, mention)
sight (n., vision, view)
site (n., location, setting)

course (n., route, direction, class)
coarse (adj., rough, made of large particles)

dew (n., small drops of moisture)
do (v., to perform, accomplish, create)
due (n., something that is owed; adj., fitting, expected; adv., exactly or directly)

die (v., to cease living)
dye (v., to color; n., coloring)

faze (v., to upset; unfazed—*not* "unphased")
phase (n., a stage of development, part)

Some investors go from "rags to **riches**"; others don't. (*Not,* **riches;**" —see page 165.)

feet (n., plural of foot)
feat (n., outstanding deed)

floe (n., large ice mass)
flow (v., to move freely; n., running water)

foreword (n., introduction to a book)
forward (adv., toward the front; adj., near the front; n., a position
 in certain sports)

forth (adv., out, forward, into view)
fourth (adj., after "third"; one quarter)

hangar (n., building for aircraft)
hanger (n., clothes hanger, a person who hangs things)

lead (rhymes with "feed": v., to guide; rhymes with "Fred": n., a metal)
led (rhymes with "Fred": v., past tense of "lead")

pair (n., two)
pare (v., to peel)
pear (n., a fruit)

peer (v., to look closely; n., an equal)
pier (n., a platform over water)

plain (adj., clear; n., flat, treeless area)
plane (n., airplane, level surface)

AGAINST THE GRAIN by Glenn Foden

pole (n., upright post, slender rod, the north and south regions of
 the earth)
poll (n., survey)

Imus and McCord correct people's **grammar**. (*Not,* **grammer**—see page 6.)

pore (v., to study with great concentration; n., tiny skin opening)
pour (v., to flow freely)

principal (n., adminstrator, money; adj., main)
principle (n., rule)

reek (v., to smell bad; n., a bad odor)
wreak (rhymes with "seek": v., to bring about or inflict)

role (n., part played by an actor; duty)
roll (v., to turn; n., a roster, a small bread loaf)

sleight (rhymes with "light": n., skill, cunning)
slight (v., to underestimate, insult, neglect; adj., meager, small)

spade (n., digging tool, playing card symbol)
spayed (v., neutered)

stationary (adj., stable, not moving)
stationery (n., writing paper)

THE FAR SIDE by Gary Larson

"Well, I've got good gnus and I've got bad gnus."

The good "gnus" is that cartoonists love homophones.

DID YOU KNOW? Words that look the same and sound the same are simply words with multiple meanings. Think of "bear": The hyperactive **bear** couldn't **bear** to hibernate all winter.

Another example is "cardinal," a word you spell and pronounce the same whether you mean the crested red bird, a Roman Catholic official, or the cardinal numbers that indicate quantity: 38, 105, 400 . . .

Some day, I'll ride a Harley. (*Not*, **someday**—see page 177.)

HOPEFULLY

The adverb "hopefully" has become a filler word. Used correctly, this word means "filled with hope."

> "Marry me, Miranda," begged Arturo **hopefully**.

Avoid "hopefully" when it doesn't have a verb to modify:

> **"Hopefully**, Taffy's fleas are finally gone," said Mrs. Wheezle. (Surely those fleas weren't filled with hope when they left!)

> *The Fix:*
> "I **hope** Taffy's fleas are finally gone," said Mrs. Wheezle.

HYPERBOLE *(See figures of speech, page 79.)*

HYPHENS *(See also compound adjectives, page 14; compound nouns, page 120; dashes, page 66; phrasals, page 130; and prefixes, page 141.)*
Hyphens (-) link words together. Use hyphens to avoid confusion.

> **smoke-free airport**   **self-help books**   **cell-phone addicts**

Use hyphens:

▶ With some prefixes, especially when the root word is capitalized.

> **self-discovery**   **ex-president**   **semi-sweet**
> **pre-Oscar party**   **pre-Christian era**   **mid-January**

▶ With blended double surnames.

> Greenfield-Martin   Hunter-Gault   Ochoa-Roberts

TIP: Alphabetize hyphenated names by the first letter of the name that appears before the hyphen.

▶ With the names of compound numbers from 21–99 and written fractions. *(See numbers, page 120.)*

> **thirty-three**   **fifty-five**   **eighty-seventh**
> **five-eighths**   **one-half**   **two-thirds**

TIP: Use figures for fractions that accompany a whole number.

> 6 $^2/_3$ 55 $^3/_4$ 178 $^1/_2$

I heard about **his** catching the crocodile. (*Not,* **him**—see page 150.)

▶ With numbers showing age or time.

> ten-year-old spelling champ
> 18- to 22-year-old undergraduates
> two- to three-year period
> 47-year marriage

▶ With highways and to designate aircraft.

I-805   DC-3   F-16

▶ With compound modifiers. (*See compound adjectives, page 14.*)

> a can't-miss putt

> The candidate's running-mate criteria reflect the growing role of minorities and women.

Alas, remembering the evolving rules of hyphenation is like trying to drive through quicksand. Hyphens don't always stick to the rules above. For example, different current dictionaries recognize both "mouthwatering" (no hyphen) and "mouth-watering" (with hyphen) as adjectives. "Work-release" has a hyphen; "workroom" does not. "Witch-hunt," yes. "Witchcraft," no.

SALLY FORTH by Greg Howard

"Re-" Words

The prefix *re-* means "again." A hyphen after the prefix can change the meaning of a word:

> Jessie **re-covered** ("covered again") the sofa herself.

> Tammy **recovered** ("got better") surprisingly fast from the flu.

Many words that start with the prefix *re-* don't require a hyphen: *recrown, redrawn, rehire, reheat,* and *repaint.* But sometimes omitting the hyphen changes the meaning of the word.

The twins talked until **3 A.M.** (*Not,* **3:00** A.M. —see page 188.)

Do you mean . . .

> "represent" (to stand for) *or* "re-present" (to present again)?
>
> "repose" (calmness) *or* "re-pose" (to pose again)?
>
> "reprove" (to rebuke) *or* "re-prove" (to prove again)?
>
> "resort" (n., vacation spot; v., to go or turn to)
>   *or* "re-sort" (to sort again)?
>
> "restrain" (to hold back) *or* "re-strain" (to strain again)?
>
> "recount" (to tell a tale) *or* "re-count" (to count again)?
> (Some dictionaries recognize "recount"—no hyphen—for "to count again.")

In one of our classes, Jason told a story that highlights the difference a hyphen can make. Away on a trip, his boss sent Jason an email asking him to resend her some information. He faxed it, then emailed her, "I **resent** it." When the boss returned, she asked him, "Jason, why did you **resent** sending me that information again?" (Jason had typed "resent" when "re-sent" would have been clearer.)

"Well-" Words

Use a hyphen when "well" appears before the noun it modifies.

well-written satire   **well-oiled machine**   **well-known person**

Faith Hill received **well-earned** praise for singing at the Oscars.

Drop the hyphen in "well-" adjectives if they follow a "to be" verb.

Praise for Faith Hill's singing at the Oscars was **well earned**.

Tricky Hyphen Issues (*See chart, page 133.*)

To hyphenate or not to hyphenate? Do you **pick up** your toys, **pick-up** your toys, or **pickup** your toys? Is it **pickup** truck, **pick-up** truck, or **pick up** truck?

The answers can be more challenging than you might think. Words are constantly evolving. Today, more and more words are losing their hyphens and becoming single words.

(Answer: You can **pick up** your toys in your **pickup** truck.)

Wylie is **vain** as a peacock. (*Not,* **vein** or **vane**—see page 189.)

General Rules *(See phrasals, page 130.)*

▶ Make most compound verbs two words. *(See phrasal verbs, page 131.)*

Back up your computer documents. (*Not*, **back-up**.)

"You **mix up** the brownie ingredients, Frog," said Toad. (*Not*, **mix-up**.)

Please **follow up** on the missing hot air balloon. (*Not*, **followup**.)

▶ Link the words in compound nouns and adjectives, either as a single word or with a hyphen.

Take this **off-ramp** for the **off-road** rally.
    (noun)   *(adjective)*

Provide **backup** for the **back-up** team.
    (noun)   *(adjective)*

TIP: While most dictionaries list the noun "backup" as a single word, a few recognize the hyphenated spelling of "back-up." Just don't use the two-word verb "back up" when you mean the noun. Write "The SWAT team called for **backup**" (*or* "back-up"), *not* "The SWAT team called for **back up**."

Hyphens: All in the Family

How do you handle words that show family relationships? Use hyphens for most relationship words, except "grand" or "step"; make those one word. Use two words (no hyphen) with "half":

sons-in-law	great-uncle	sister-in-law
grandmother	stepbrother	stepmom
half brother	half sister	

DID YOU KNOW? Many job titles, such as "attorney-at-law," are hyphenated. Others, such as "editor in chief" and "commander in chief" (or "Commander in Chief"), are not hyphenated. With other compound words, don't be surprised if you find hyphen disagreements from dictionary to dictionary. Choose one style—and be consistent.

Note that Americans tend to hyphenate much less than the British, Canadians, and Australians. That explains the inconsistencies found in the English language around the world.

This type of gridlock is unprecedented. (*Not*, **These type**—see page 154.)

IDIOMS

CROCK by Bill Rechin and Don Wilder

Idioms are expressions that have understood meanings, which are often figurative rather than literal. While native speakers take the meanings of idioms for granted, they can confuse people just learning English or anyone not familiar with the reference.

"The gerbil kicked the bucket" doesn't mean the little furry thing is kicking a tiny bucket; this idiom means that the gerbil died. People often use idioms in casual speech and dialogue. Many idioms have been in use so long that they have become clichés. Use idioms sparingly.

Do you know these common idioms?

Hey, Savion, **break a leg**! (From theater: "Good luck!")

I'm **burning the midnight oil**. (I'm staying up late.)

JUMP START by Robb Armstrong

Lawyers follow the **tenets** of the law. (*Not*, **tenants**—see page 187.)

Melissa was **wiped out** after the twelve-hour American Bar exam. (She was exhausted.)

Erika, **it's up to you**. (You decide what to do now.)

The news went **in one ear and out the other**. (The person wasn't listening.)

What's the good word? What's up? How's it going? (What is happening in your life?)

What's up with that? (What does that mean?)

She really **poured it on thick**. (She exaggerated.)

Sandals **sell like hotcakes** in the summer. (They sell well.)

Please **cut me some slack**. (Ease up on me.)

Ruthie May has a **pie-in-the-sky attitude**. (She's a dreamer.)

Charlotte Church's voice is **out of this world**. (She sings really well.)

Chip and Cathy are **on the same wavelength**. (They think alike.)

Don't bite off more than you can chew. (Don't take on more tasks than you can handle.)

Michelle's **eyes were bigger than her stomach**. (She took more food than she could eat.)

Ms. Mahany, your oven's **good to go**. (It's fixed.)

My ex-girlfriends? **Don't go there**. (I don't want to talk about them.)

Pet rocks were just a **flash in the pan**. (They were a momentary fad.)

Martina Hingis **had her day in the sun**. (People recognized her achievements.)

Coaches sometimes **pull strings** for players. (Coaches may bend academic standards.)

Two easily confused idioms:

champing at the bit (being impatient) (*not* **chomping**)

stomping ground or **grounds** (familiar territory) (*not* **stamping ground**)

Life is short. Eat **dessert** first. (*Not,* **desert**—see page 69.)

Both "champ" and "chomp" mean "to chew upon noisily," but "champing" is the idiom. While "stamping ground" appears in most American dictionaries, it's primarily British English and used much less frequently than "stomping ground."

Readers were **champing at the bit** to read J.K. Rowlings's next book.

George was back in New Orleans, his old **stomping grounds**.

IN THE BLEACHERS by Steve Moore

www.uexpress.com
© 2000 Universal Press Syndicate

"This is not fair! How can they expect us to compete if we're not on a level playing field?"

Sports Talk

Sports talk has become part of business settings, as well as everyday life.

That idea is **off the wall**. (That idea is unusual.)

They're **out in left field**. (They're out of touch.)

Right off the bat, the team cooperated. (From the start, the team cooperated.)

This is **straight from the horse's mouth**. (This information came directly from the source.)

Let's **touch base** Tuesday. (Let's contact each other on Tuesday.)

Further clues led them to the missing marbles. (*Not,* **farther**—see page 78.)

It's a **slam dunk**. (It's certain.)

Don't **drop the ball**. (Do your part.)

Let's **get the ball rolling**. (Let's begin.)

Hold your horses! (Wait a minute!)

You're **in the ballpark**. (Your ideas or numbers are reasonable.)

Bull's eye! (Perfect!)

The **ball's in your court**. (It's your responsibility.)

Take a crack at it. (You try doing this.)

Step up to the plate. (Take your turn.)

Work Talk

Some idioms are specific to the work environment.

Eric's **beefing up** his résumé. (He's making his résumé stronger.)

What's the **bottom line**? (How much will this cost?)

Climb the corporate ladder. (Take a series of jobs or promotions leading to upper management jobs.)

She's **hit the glass ceiling**. (She's encountered hidden barriers to advancement.)

The company is **downsizing**. (It's cutting back on personnel.)

The company's **going public**. (It's offering stock to the public.)

They're **letting him go**. (They're firing him.)

Charlie's **crunching the numbers**. (He's analyzing the financial situation.)

We're **playing phone tag**. (We're missing each other's phone calls.)

Start **thinking outside the box**. (Think of new, creative, or unusual ideas.)

What's your **turnaround time**? (How fast can you complete the job?)

She works **24/7**. (She works long hours: 24 hours a day, 7 days a week.)

We finished **J.I.T.** (We finished "just in time" to meet our deadline.)

Dudley **honed** his couch potato skills. (*Not*, homed—see page 87.)

IMPERATIVE MOOD (*See verbs, page 197.*)

IMPLY, INFER

"To imply" is "to hint at, to suggest." "To infer" is "to deduce or conclude."

> The plumber **implied** that Satchel's rubber ducky had clogged the toilet.

> Desirée **inferred** from Roger's face that he was hiding something.

INCOMPLETE SENTENCES

In formal writing, use complete sentences. But when speaking informally, it's fine to use incomplete sentences: "See you," "In a minute," "Later, Gator," or "If I have time."

> "Me? Win the lottery? Fat chance!"

An incomplete sentence may be a comma splice, a fragment, or a run-on.

Comma Splices

When you use a comma where a period or a semicolon is needed, you make an error called a "comma splice." You're accidentally using commas to splice two complete sentences together.

> *Comma Splices:*
> Buckle up, it's the law.

> I saw you there, Steve was with you.

> Daisy pouted, she usually does.

Three Ways to Fix Comma Splices

1. Split the comma splice into two separate sentences.

   > Buckle up! It's the law.

2. Join the two sentences with a semicolon.

   > I saw you there; Steve was with you.

3. Insert a conjunction between the two sentences.

   > Daisy pouted**, as** she usually does.

Mailbox: **The Keeneys.** (*Not,* **The Keeney's**—see page 136.)

Sentence Fragments (*See dependent clauses, page 50 and subject, page 183*)
Putting a capital at the beginning and a period at the end of a string of words doesn't always create a complete sentence. Fragments are incomplete sentences, such as stranded dependent clauses.

My party was great. **Birthday streamers everywhere!**

Playing in the mud. The toddler was covered from head to toe.

I'll call Grandma. **If you want me to.**

Wild, woolly Texas. It's known for its longhorn cattle.

"Heinrich proposed. **While I was bowling.**"

Siraj planned to shoot the rapids next weekend. **His life long dream.** (The noun phrase is missing a verb: It's a fragment.)

A fragment is easy to fix. Either join it to a complete sentence or turn it into a complete sentence.

My party was great, especially the birthday streamers everywhere.

The toddler was covered from head to toe from playing in the mud.

I'll call Grandma if you want me to.

Wild, woolly Texas is known for its longhorn cattle.

"While I was bowling, Heinrich proposed."

Siraj planned to shoot the rapids next weekend. It was his lifelong dream.

Run-On Sentences
Run-on sentences don't know where to stop. They happen when two independent clauses don't have a conjunction or the punctuation to correctly join them. (Run-on sentences have other names: "fused sentences" *or* "comma faults.")

Run-On:
She entered in a gown and cape he followed in a bunny outfit.

The dog **dragged** his feather bed outside. (*Not,* **drug**—see page 203.)

Three Ways to Fix Run-On Sentences

1. Split the run-on sentence into two separate sentences.

   She entered in a gown and cape. **He** followed in a bunny outfit.

2. Join the two sentences with a semicolon.

   She entered in a gown and cape**;** he followed in a bunny outfit.

3. Insert a conjunction between the two sentences.

   She entered in a gown and cape**, and** he followed in a bunny outfit.

DID YOU KNOW? Used sparingly, incomplete sentences can add emphasis in informal writing. For example, "She can really pump iron. And how!" Just be sure that your meaning is clear.

INDEFINITE PRONOUNS *(See pages 25-26, 151-153.)*

INFER *(See imply, infer, page 99.)*

INFINITIVES *(See verbs, page 192.)*

INITIALISMS *(See abbreviations, page 9, and acronyms, page 14.)*

An initialism is an abbreviation that you pronounce letter by letter:

ASAP	as soon as possible
ATM	automated teller machine
CDC	Center for Disease Control
CEO	chief executive officer
FYI	for your information
IPO	initial public offering
IRS	Internal Revenue Service
ISBN	International Standard Book Number
MVP	most valuable player
NPR	National Public Radio
SASE	self-addressed stamped envelope
SPF	sun protection factor
SUV	sports utility vehicle
UMW	United Mine Workers
UN	United Nations

The Beatles strode **onstage;** fans squealed. (*Not,* **onstage,**—see page 99.)

BEETLE BAILEY by Mort Walker
Make certain your readers understand the meanings of initialisms by spelling out the words the first time they are used.

Our new **chief financial officer (CFO)** is a real Scrooge.

INTERJECTIONS
Interjections express outbursts of feeling: "Wow!" "Phooey!" "Drat!" "Zoinks!" They can be part of a sentence or separate.

Use a comma after a mild interjection:

Rats, my cell phone's dead.

Use an exclamation point after a strong interjection:

"**Bummer!** The swordfish got away," yelled Chris.

Save interjections for speech and informal writing.

INTERROGATIVE VERBS *(See verbs, page 197.)*

INTRANSITIVE VERBS *(See verbs, page 192.)*

IRREGULAR VERBS *(See verbs, page 202.)*

ITALICS *(See abbreviations, page 9, and quotation marks, page 163.)*
Thanks to word processors, you can now italicize with a keystroke. (If you don't have access to a computer, indicate italics by underlining: <u>The Wind in the Willows</u>.)

The first song Johnny Mathis **sang** was "Misty." (*Not,* **sung**—see page 205.)

Use italics:

▶ For scientific names.

> *Tyrannosaurus rex* (a dinosaur)
> *Condylura cristata* (a star-nosed mole)
> *Staphylococcus* (a bacterium that causes boils)
> *Longisquama* (a mouse-sized prehistoric animal)

TIP: Capitalize only the first word of these scientific names.

▶ For emphasis.

> He *did* bring me flowers; but I'm allergic to ragweed.

▶ To highlight an example.

> The term *to get away with murder* defined the defendant's case. (You can also enclose the phrase in quotation marks: "to get away with murder.")

▶ For screenplay directions, to show how a character should speak a line.

> Kermit (*innocently*): It's not that easy being green.

▶ For titles. *(See quotation marks, page 163.)*
As a rule of thumb, use quotation marks for titles of shorter works, italics for longer works.

> **Artistic works:** *Mona Lisa* (Leonardo da Vinci)
> **Books:** *Fooling with Words: A Celebration of Poets and Their Craft* (Bill Moyers)
> **Cartoon strips:** *For Better or for Worse* (Lynn Johnston)
> **Cartoon shows:** *Arthur*
> **CDs and DVDs:** *Noche de cuatro lunas* (Julio Iglesias)
> **Journals:** *JAMA* (*Journal of the American Medical Association*)
> **Long poems:** *Evangeline* (Henry Wadsworth Longfellow)
> **Magazines:** *Wired*
> **Movies:** *Walk the Line*
> **Musical works:** *1812 Overture* (Peter Ilich Tchaikovsky)
> **Newspapers:** *Arizona Sun, Washington Post, New York Times, Detroit Free Press*
> **Plays, musicals:** *Fosse*
> **Radio shows and series:** *Holder Overnight* (CJAD, Montreal, Peter Anthony Holder); *Fresh Air* (NPR, Terry Gross)
> **TV shows and series:** *Friends, A&E Biography*

Elise's master's degree reads **Fall 2000**. (*Not,* **Fall, 2000**—see page 48.)

▶ For words from other languages.
Use italics for foreign phrases that are not yet common in English.

bon ami	*pièce de resistance*
c'est magnifique	*mea culpa*
c'est fini	*feng shui*
E pluribus unum	*Hasta la vista,* Baby

Some foreign words (shish kebab, en masse, café au lait, and maven, for instance) have been used so often that they are no longer italicized. Set these words in Roman type (standard type), not *italics.*

More Italics Tips

▶ Italicize names of ships, submarines, airplanes, spacecraft, and satellites.

Grand Princess	*Air Force One*
Sojourner	the space shuttle *Endeavor*

Don't italicize an abbreviation, numeral, type, or class before or after a specific ship or spacecraft name.

HMS *Pinafore*   *Voyager* 2 **(spacecraft)**

▶ If you make an italicized word plural or possessive, don't italicize the *s* or *'s.*

Rick had a stack of *Surfer Magazine*s.

Business and financial sectors dominate *Forbes*'s demographics.

▶ If a question mark is not part of the italicized text, use Roman type for the question mark.

Have you seen my copy of *Latina*?

▶ If a question mark is part of the italicized text, italicize it.

Richard Nelson Bolles wrote the bestseller *What Color Is Your Parachute?*

Do not use a period after the question mark: The question mark serves as end punctuation.

▶ Do not italicize architectural works or natural sites, such as the Empire State Building or the Grand Canyon.

A mouse was featured in **Stuart Little**. (*Not,* "Stuart Little."—see page 103.)

IT'S, ITS (*See contractions, page 190, and possessive pronouns, page 149.*)
Does the dog wag **it's** tail or **its** tail? (See below.)

It's

The apostrophe in "it's" indicates a contraction, a combination of two
words with one or more letters missing. "It's" = "it is."

> Look at that clear blue sky—**it's** another day in paradise.

> On the Wall Street trading floor, **it's** important to carry Tums.

Its

"Its," a possessive pronoun, shows ownership. The **s** is part of the word. No
apostrophe is needed.

> The movie *Dinosaur* wowed viewers with **its** special effects.

> The aardvark inhaled **its** lunch of ants and termites.

MNEMONIC (MEMORY AID): Possessive **its** never sp**lits.** Don't use an apostrophe
with "its"—you don't use an apostrophe with "his" or "hers."
To test whether to use "it's" or "its," say, "it is." If the sentence makes
sense, use the contraction "it's." Otherwise, use the possessive "its."
Does the dog wag "it is" tail? No, so use "its": The dog wags **its** tail.

J

JIBE, JIVE

"To jibe" is a verb meaning "to agree" or, in sailing, "to shift direction."
"Jive" is a noun meaning "swing or jazz music."

> Their versions of the showdown at Tombstone didn't **jibe.**

> Musicians at the Wild Note play **jive** every night.

(These words have other meanings, too. Check your dictionary.)

Karen's lawn-mowing business made money. (*Not,* **Karens'**—see page 139.)

L

LATIN PLURALS (*See also plurals, page 133, and prefixes, page 141.*)
Even if you've never studied Latin, you know many Latin words. *Aqua* is
"water" (aquarium, Aquaman). *Stella* is "star" (constellation, stellar job).
With some words of Latin origin, just follow the English rule of adding an *s*
or *es* to form plurals:

> forum, forums (*not* fora)

> thesaurus, thesauruses (*not* thesauri) (This Latin word is actually
> borrowed from Greek.)

THE BIG E: Some words have kept the Latin form of the plural. The words
"alumnus" and "alumni" (rhymes with "pie") refer to male high school or
college graduates and to mixed groups of graduates (male and female).
Don't use "alumnuses." The words "alumna" and "alumnae" ("uh lum´ **nee**,"
as in "**Ca**esar") refer to female graduates. Don't use "alumnas." Informally,
you can also shorten "alumnus" to "alum" for male or female grads. Accent
the second syllable: "uh lum´."

The word "phenomenon" is singular. The word "phenomena" (*not* phe-
nomenons) is plural.

The word "criterion" is singular. The word "criteria" (*not* criterions)
is plural.

Right
One criterion—not breaking—governed the Egg Drop Contest.

Wrong
One criteria—not breaking—governed the Egg Drop Contest.

? **Why?** "One" is singular. Use the singular "criterion," not the plural
"criteria."

DID YOU KNOW? The word "species" is a Latin noun meaning "a distinct
kind." It has the same form in the singular and plural. (There is a word
"specie," but it means "coin.")

The Data, Datum Conundrum
Controversy reigns in the "datum, data" debate. Technically, the Latin
word "datum" is singular: It means a single piece of information. "Data" is
plural: It means pieces of information, or facts.

My roommate and I pull all-nighters. (*Not,* My roommate and **me**—see page 148.)

But does "data" take a plural verb or a singular verb? The answer can be "both"! Use a singular verb (such as "is," "renders," "makes," or "shows") with "data" when you mean an amount of "information" taken as a whole:

> This **data gives** credence to our theory. (*It* gives.)

> The nutritional **data supports** our rutabaga regimen. (*It* supports.)

Use a plural verb (such as "are," "render," "make," or "show") with "data" in academic or scientific writing, especially when referring to separate amounts of evidence.

> These **data support** the recent ADA guidelines for daily calcium intake. (*They* support.)

TIP: Today, you hear "datum" about as often as pigs fly. As for "data," your best bet is to consider the rest of the sentence.

LAY, LIE

JUMP START by Robb Armstrong

"To lay" is to place. "To lie" is to recline.

TIP: Hens **lay** (eggs!). People **lie**. (*For details on "lay" and "lie," see verbs, page 194.*)

LEGAL WRITING (*See ampersand, page 28, and commas, page 54.*)
Law professors are teaching students the art of reducing puffed-up language to make laws, statutes, propositions, and other legal documents more clear.

As I said, swimming is life. (*Not,* **Like I said**—see page 37.)

JUMP START by Robb Armstrong

Simplifying Legalese

Law students are learning to write less-complicated sentences and find simpler terms for phrases, such as *whereas the party of the first part, aforementioned, insofar as, herein, heretofore, hereinbefore,* and *hereinafter.*

> *Legalese Version:*
> By reason of the fact that the witness had disappeared, the trial was postponed.

> *Simplified Version:*
> The judge postponed the trial because the witness had disappeared.

Paying Attention to Punctuation *(See commas, page 54.)*

In law, the placement of a comma, colon, or semicolon can make a big difference in the interpretation of a law or in drafting other legal documents, such as wills.

Without the serial comma, Phil receives a bonanza:

> I bequeath all my worldly goods to Phil, Lil **and** Will. (Phil gets half, while Lil and Will split the other half.)

In the serial-comma version, Phil's share is reduced:

> I bequeath all my worldly goods to Phil, Lil**, and** Will. (They each. receive a third.)

Clarifying Jury Instructions

In California, a group of judges, lawyers, linguists, and laypeople is rewriting jury instructions in plain, simple English. Here's a sampling:

I am **averse** to fried crickets. (*Not,* **adverse**—see page 21.)

Current: Failure of recollection is common. Innocent misrecollection is not uncommon.
Proposed: People sometimes honestly forget things or make mistakes about what they remember.

Current: Circumstantial evidence
Proposed: Indirect evidence

Current: Preponderance of the evidence
Proposed: More likely true than not true

Associate Justice Carol A. Corrigan of the California state Court of Appeals says, "Why not explain the law to jurors in language that they understand?" Her rationale for simplicity applies to all aspects of law.

LEND, LOAN

MOMMA by Mell Lazarus

The Grammar Patrol still treats "lend" as a verb and "loan" as a noun. (Keeping this lend/loan distinction is probably a losing battle.)

"**Lend** me your yacht for the weekend, please, please, please?" wheedled Danny.

"I think not. Get a **loan** for your own yacht," retorted Nigel.

LET'S, LETS

The word "let's" is a contraction, meaning "let us."

"**Let's** go to Sea World," said Chloë.

The verb "lets" is the third person singular form of the verb "to let."

Judith **lets** spiders live indoors, as long as they don't crawl into beds.

At halftime, over **5,000** toilets flushed citywide. (*Not,* 5000—see page 121.)

LIGHTED, LIT

Use "lighted" as an adjective. Use "lit" as the simple past tense of "to light."

A **lighted** candle led Angus to the castle.

One thousand lights **lit** the White House Christmas tree.

LIKE *(See as, like, page 37; fillers, page 80; and similes, page 176.)*

LIKE, SUCH AS

Both "like" and "such as" are correct when used to introduce examples. "Such as" suggests a more formal tone. Use a comma before "like" or " such as" when a list with commas follows:

She adored Italian food, **like** antipasto, ravioli, and lasagna.

Kenneth "Babyface" Edmonds has written songs for many performers, **such as** Madonna, Eric Clapton, and Whitney Houston.

LIKELY

When the word "likely" is used as an adverb, it needs a modifier, such as *most, very, quite,* or *rather.*

 Right
I will **most likely** dine with Denzel Washington.

 Wrong
I will **likely** dine with Denzel Washington.

? **Why?** Don't use the adverb "likely" alone. Add a modifier.

The same goes for other often-heard uses of "likely." Say, "**Most likely**, she'll wing-walk this Sunday," *not* "**Likely** she'll wing-walk this Sunday." Say, "Jill will **very likely** find her purse," *not* "Jill **will likely** find her purse."

You can use "likely" alone when it is used as a predicate adjective (one joined by a linking verb to the subject).

Rain **is likely** to fall Tuesday.
(linking verb) (predicate adjective)

LINKING VERBS *(See verbs, page 196.)*

Simon **piqued** Bernadine's interest. (*Not,* **peeked** or **peaked**—see page 127.)

LITERAL, LITERALLY *(See figures of speech, page 79.)*

"Literal," an adjective, means "word for word," exact. "Literally," an adverb, means "in a literal, not a figurative, sense."

> The **literal** meaning of *carte blanche* is "blank card."

> During the quake, I was **literally** shaking.

👍 **Right**
Election officials **literally** worked night and day.

👎 **Wrong**
Election officials **literally** drowned in chads.

❓ **Why?** "Literally" is often not needed or used incorrectly. Election officials *can* work long, long, hours, but they wouldn't really drown in tiny pieces of paper.

LOSE, LOOSE

The verb "to lose" (rhymes with "shoes") means "to fail to find," or "to be deprived of." "Loose" (rhymes with "goose") is an adjective meaning "free," or "not tight."

> I **lose** my glasses constantly.

> Name of an Alaskan store chain: Moose on the **Loose**.

> The elastic in Dudley's jogging pants came **loose**.

MNEMONIC (MEMORY AID): "Loose" and "tight" both have five letters.

MALAPROPISMS

John Dryden coined the word "malapropism" in the sixteenth century, to mean inappropriate word combinations. The character Mrs. Malaprop in *The Rivals,* a 1775 play by Richard Sheridan, helped popularize this eponymous term. Mrs. Malaprop had a way of *almost* getting her words right. The results were often hilarious—"alligator" for "allegory" or "Lead the way and we'll precede" (should be "proceed"). Barbara Kingsolver had one of her *Poisonwood Bible* characters, Rachel Price, specialize in malapropisms.

With regard to your order, Silly Putty is sold out. (*Not,* **With regards to**—see page 171.)

"Already I was heavy-hearted in my soul for the things in life I have took [*sic*] for **granite** (**granted**)."

Be on the lookout for malapropisms.

Olivia's suitor was driving **erotically** (**erratically**).

Tess is known on campus as a **rebel** (**rabble**) rouser.

President Carter made a **conscience** (**conscious**) decision to support Habitat for Humanity.

For many years, Mr. Quigley had remained **monotonous** (**monogamous**).

My **prospective** (**perspective**) differs greatly from yours.

I haven't been living in a **vacuum cleaner** (**vacuum**) all year.

MARINADE, MARINATE

A marinade is a spiced liquid used before cooking to season or tenderize · foods. The verb "to marinate" means "to soak in a marinade."

Use Freddy's Pineapple **Marinade** to **marinate** the swordfish.

MEASUREMENT (*See numbers, page 120.*)

MEDAL, METAL, METTLE

A "medal" is an award. "Metal" refers to elements such as copper or iron, often combined to form alloys. "Mettle" means "courage, fortitude, strength of character."

Bill framed his uncle's World War II **medals**.

The idiom "Put the pedal to the **metal**" means "Drive fast! Slam that accelerator to the floor of the car!"

A magazine article about the Tour de France bicycle race used a play on words in its headline:

"Put the Pedal to the **Mettle**" (*Sports Illustrated,* July 24, 2000)

MEDIOCRE, MUNDANE

The adjective "mediocre" means "undistinguished, ordinary." "Mundane" means "of this world, not spiritual; practical or commonplace."

Zonk's and Syd's views about body piercing **jibed**. (*Not*, **jived**—see page 105.)

Due to inferior brandy, Ida's Cherries Jubilee was **mediocre**.

Bored with **mundane** housework, Priscilla took up the harp.

MEMENTO

MUTTS by Patrick McDonnell

A "memento" is a keepsake.

Her grandmother's locket was a treasured **memento**.

The word "memento" is often misspelled and mispronounced as "momento."

METAPHORS *(See also figures of speech, page 79, and similes, page 176.)*

GET FUZZY by Darby Conley

Bucky's dripping faucet, above, doesn't signal a need for a plumber, but some deeper theme in the movie they are watching. (Bucky also throws in a lovely malapropism: "melted flower" for "metaphor.")

"Then **Julian says**, 'It's over, Snookums.' " (*Not*, **Julian goes**—see page 182.)

Metaphors are figures of speech that compare, making two very different things seem similar. One thing is used as a symbol for another, such as an empty street for loneliness.

Metaphors say that one thing *is* another thing.

> **Annalisa** is a **dolphin** in the ocean, diving through the waves.

> **Henry** was a **mule** about changing his mind.

MIXED METAPHORS
Mixed metaphors awkwardly combine parts of two familiar metaphors, which can confuse the reader.

> **Throw down the gauntlet to the wolves.** (This is a mix of "throw down the gauntlet" and "throw someone to the wolves.")

> **Don't spill wild oats.** (This is a mix of "don't spill the beans" and "sow wild oats.")

MODE, MOOD
The noun "mode" means a way or style of doing something. The noun "mood" means "state of mind."

> Bentley, in taxpaying **mode**, riffled through a shoebox of receipts.

> Serena was in a foul **mood** after Hernando stood her up.

MODIFIERS (*See adjectives, page 14; adverbs, page 17; clauses, page 50; dangling participial phrases, page 65; and phrases, page 133.*)
Modifiers describe, limit, or qualify another word. They can be adjectives, adverbs, phrases, or clauses.

> **squeaky** wheel
> (*adjective*)

> grinned **naughtily**
> (*adverb*)

> Running from the python, I fell.
> (*participial phrase*)

> The man who came to dinner stayed for years.
> (*clause*)

Chocolates on the pillow are a **bonus**. (*Not,* **added bonus**—see page 169.)

Misplaced Modifiers

Misplaced modifiers result when words or phrases are too far from the words they modify or describe.

> She had read why the *Titanic* sank **in the morning paper**. (The *Titanic* sank in the morning paper?)

> **Until proven innocent**, I will hold Dilbert guilty. (Who is guilty, "I" or "Dilbert"?)

> Paleobiologists search for dinosaurs **with computers**. (Dinosaurs with laptops?)

> **When he was in the second grade**, my father told me he learned to read. (A seven-year-old dad?)

Modifier Placement Affects Meaning

With some modifiers, such as "only" and "not," placement in a sentence affects the meaning:

> **Only** I have eyes for you. (No one else likes you.)

> I have **only** eyes for you. (Not ears, mouth, feet . . .)

> I have eyes **only** for you. (You're the one for me, Babe!)

MOOD *(See mode, mood, page 114, and verbs, page 196.)*

N

NEGATIVES

Like insistent two-year-olds, negative words say "no" or "not." Common negatives are *no, not, nothing, no one* (*not* "noone"), *nowhere* (*not* "nowheres"), *nobody*.

Making Positive Verbs Negative

You can make most positive verbs negative by pairing them with "do not" or the contraction "don't."

Audrey's list: **walking** stick, hiking boots, laptop. (*Not*, list: **Walking**—see page 53.)

Positive	Negative
whine	don't whine
sky dive	do not sky dive
lollygag	do not lollygag
stare	don't stare

With forms of the verb "to be," only the negative "not" is needed, not the word "do."

I **am not** a crook.

They **weren't** great chefs.

You **are not** Ricky Martin.

DID YOU KNOW? The Johnny Mercer song from the 40s that said to "accentuate the positive" had the right idea. The positive "Remember your ticket" is stronger than the negative "Don't forget your ticket."

Double Negatives

WIZARD OF ID by Brant Parker and Johnny Hart

This cartoon parent uses a double negative: "ain't" and "nuthin'." (And "ain't" ain't proper, anyway.)

When you accidentally pair two negatives, you create a **double negative**. Double negatives are a definite "no-no"! Along with the negative words listed above, these adverbs are negative: "barely," "hardly," and "scarcely."

Say, "There aren't any cookies left" or "There are no cookies left," *not* "There aren't no cookies left." Use only one negative: "aren't" (for "are not") or "no," but not both.

Art's **regimen** includes a daily bike ride. (*Not,* **regiment**—see page 171.)

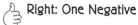 **Right: One Negative**

 Wrong: Double Negatives

Right: One Negative	Wrong: Double Negatives
I **don't** have any Cheese Puffs.	I **don't** have **no** Cheese Puffs.
I can **hardly** wait.	I **can't hardly** wait.
Henry **won't** go anywhere!	Henry **won't** go **nowhere!**
Timmy could **scarcely** speak.	Timmy **couldn't scarcely** speak.
They take **no** guff.	They **don't** take **no** guff.

Songwriters love double negatives:

"**Don't** want **nothin'** from ya, Baby . . ."

"I **can't** get **no** lovin' anymore . . ."

Negative Prefixes

Some prefixes are negative. When joined to a word, they can mean "not." Examples are *dis-, il-, im-, in-, ir-, non-,* and **un-**.

disagreeable (not agreeable)   immortal (not mortal)
irreplaceable (not replaceable)   unappealing (not appealing)
illogical (not logical)   inefficient (not efficient)
nonaggressive (not aggressive)

Beware of creating your own substandard negative words:

unexperienced (should be "inexperienced")
displeasant (should be "unpleasant")
unimpossible (should be "possible"—two negatives make a positive!)
unseparable (should be "inseparable")
unefficient (should be "inefficient")

Use a hyphen with **non-** only when it precedes a proper noun or adjective, as in, "non-Catholic denomination."

Some prefixes are joined to the word; others are separated from the word with a hyphen. Consult your dictionary. (*See hyphens, page 91, and prefixes, page 141.*)

DID YOU KNOW? "I **couldn't** care less" uses the negative "not" correctly. If you say, "I could care less," you would mean that it *is* possible for you to care less than you already do.

Crystal is **lying** down. (*Not,* **laying**—see page 194.)

NEGLIGENT, NEGLIGIBLE

The adjective "negligent" means "guilty of neglect." "Negligible" means "so small, not worth considering."

Fabio was **negligent** in forgetting Valentine's Day.

Response to my mismatched socks ad was **negligible**.

NOBEL, NOBLE

The Nobel Prizes are the annual honorary prizes named for Alfred Nobel. "Noble" means "aristocratic, imposing."

Barbara McClintock won a **Nobel** Prize in 1983.

The unsung work of literacy tutors is a **noble** undertaking.

NON SEQUITUR

"Non sequitur" is Latin for "it does not follow." Use the term when one bit of information doesn't logically follow what came before it, or a conclusion is not based on the facts.

Customer: "I'd like to buy some African violets."

Clerk's response: "Kitty litter is on sale today."

NOUNS (*See capitals, page 45; collective nouns, page 51; plurals, page 133; and predicate nouns, page 141.*)
Nouns are "namers." They are some of the first words we learn: *dog, cat, blanket, bottle,* and *cookie.* Words like *a, an, the, that, this, these,* and *those* will lead you to nouns.

the CPU   a jalopy
an ambulance   these raccoons

Or, look for **ness**, **tion**, and **ity** word endings. These endings signal that the word is a noun.

goodness   celebration   electricity

Nouns can be **singular**, meaning "one."

jet   soda   sardine
tax   patch   flurry

On **December 20, 1969,** they wed. (*Not,* **December 20 1969**—see page 68.)

Nouns can be **plural**, meaning "more than one." Plurals are usually formed by adding *s* or *es*. (If a noun ends in *y*, change the *y* to *i* and add *es*.)

jets	sodas	sardines
taxes	patches	flurries

Some nouns keep the same form, whether they are singular or plural.

elk	pants	sheep
moose	fish	deer

Common and Proper Nouns

▶ **Common nouns** are general, not specific. They name people, places, things, qualities, ideas, emotions. Don't capitalize common nouns.

People: actor, chef, designer, activist, musician, writer
Places: city, country, beach, stadium, museum
Things: piano, shampoo, computer, car, ocelot
Qualities or ideas: democracy, investment, cooperation, truth
Emotions: love, hate, grief, anger, relief, joy

▶ **Proper nouns** name specific or unique people, places, and things. These include continents, months of the year, days of the week, holidays, and other specific entities. Begin proper nouns with a capital letter:

People: Tom Cruise, Wolfgang Puck, Donna Karan, Scott Joplin, Rosemary Wells
Places: Australia, Waikiki Beach, Santa Cruz Island, the Upper Peninsula
Things: Steinway, Neutrogena, Mac OS, Cadillac, the Getty Museum, Manhattan
Continents: Africa, Antarctica, Asia, Australia, Europe, North America, South America
Months, days: April, December, Tuesday, Sunday
Holidays: Hanukkah, Thanksgiving, St. Patrick's Day

Noun Placement: Before or After Verbs

Nouns can appear before or after verbs.

Giraffes don't need **ladders** to reach their dinners.
(noun)   *(verb)*   *(noun)*

Michael Crichton wrote ***Jurassic Park***.
(noun)   *(verb)*   *(noun)*

A flock of crows **descends** on the statue. (*Not,* **descend**—see page 51.)

119

Compound Nouns (*See hyphens, page 91.*)

A **compound noun** is two or more nouns working together. These noun combinations can be written as separate words, joined with a hyphen, or closed (one word). Check a current dictionary for correct spelling.

▶ Some compound nouns are written as separate words.

ballet dancer	group therapy
football player	safety deposit box

▶ Some compound nouns are linked with hyphens.

son-in-law	pay-per-view	court-martial

▶ Some compound nouns are closed (no hyphen, no space).

barbell	bagpipe	lawbreaker
beeline	ladybug	storyteller

NUMBER (*See pronouns, page 147, and verbs, page 199.*)

Pronouns and verbs have "number": They can be singular or plural. The forms of pronouns and verbs change, according to their number.

NUMBER, AMOUNT (*See amount, number, page 28.*)

NUMBERS (NUMERALS) (*See dates, page 68.*)

Here are some number tips:

▶ When should you spell out numbers, and when should you use numerals? Sources vary. Everyone agrees to spelling out the numbers from one to nine.

three toads	nine trumpet players

Many usage experts say to use numerals (10, 20, etc.), not words (ten, twenty, etc.), for the numbers 10 to 99 and above. Others say you can use words. (Take your pick—just be consistent.)

76 trombones (*or* **seventy-six** trombones)
150 guests (*or* **one hundred fifty** guests)
600 appetizers (*or* **six hundred** appetizers)
4,000 golf balls (*or* **four thousand** golf balls)

Superman scrutinized **an article** about Kryptonite. (*Not*, **a article**—see page 35.)

Some science and technical writers use numerals for all numbers.

TIP: When mixing a low numeral with a high numeral, use either numerals or words for both:

> *Nitty-Gritty Grammar* is for anyone from **10** to **110**.

> The Ping-Pong rematch will take from **five** to **twelve** hours.

▶ If a sentence contains more than two numerals, use numerals for all.

> Buy **8** go-carts, **175** light sticks, and **1,200** bottles of bubbles.

▶ Put a comma between unrelated numbers, or spell out the first number when two numbers appear in succession.

> By 1900, **170** people populated Marine Hills, Minnesota.

> Then ten 30-year-olds ran across the field.

▶ To avoid confusion, say "zero" not "oh" when saying numbers aloud.

> *Serial Number M6G407:*
> "The serial number is "Em, six, gee, four, **zero,** seven."

> *Area Code 760:*
> "The area code is seven, six, **zero.**"

▶ Use a comma separator with numbers that tell how many. (Commas separate the hundreds, thousands, millions, and so on.)

> 2,483 Hawaiian T-shirts
> 6,000,000 invading ants

▶ Do not use a comma when indicating a year.

> The **1968 Mustang** was a beauty. (*Not,* 1968, Mustang.)

> The stock market crashed in the year **1929**. (*Not,* the year, **1929**.)

▶ Don't begin a sentence with a numeral.
Write "**Fifty-seven** golf balls landed in our yard," *not* "**57** golf balls landed in our yard."

▶ Don't use the conjunction "and" or hyphens if writing out numbers in the hundreds and thousands:

> Four hundred eleven vintage cars entered the Concours d'Élegance.

My soybean angel food cake didn't **rise**. (*Not,* **raise**—see page 195.)

▶ Feet or foot?
English can be mystifying. You say that a six-**foot** fence is six **feet** tall.

DID YOU KNOW? Math terms, such as shortened versions of "inch," "foot," and "mile," are now considered symbols, not abbreviations. With these customary English units, write "in," "ft," and "mi"—use no periods. In text, spell out these words.

O

OBJECTS

The English language has four kinds of objects: direct objects, indirect objects, object complements, and objects of prepositions.

Direct Objects

Once you know the subject and verb of a sentence, ask "whom" or "what" the subject is acting upon. A word (or words) that answers that question is a **direct object**: an object that receives the action of the verb. Only transitive verbs take direct objects. (*See transitive and intransitive verbs, page 192.*) ·

> Barbara Walters **interviews celebrities**.
> (*verb*)   (*direct object*)

Barbara Walters interviews *whom*? "Celebrities." The noun "celebrities" is the direct object of the verb "interviews."

> Celine Dion **has sold** 100 million **albums**.
> (*verb*)   (*direct object*)

Celine Dion has sold *what*? "Albums." The noun "albums," plus its adjective, "100 million," is the direct object of the verb "has sold."

Spiderman **throws** his web. (*Not,* **throw**—see page 26.)

Indirect Objects

Objects can also be indirect. **Indirect objects** always fall between a verb and a direct object. They tell you "to whom," "to what," "for whom," or "for what" the action is done.

> Stephen King **gives charities millions**. (Gives millions *to what?*)
> (verb)(indirect object)(direct object)

The direct object of the verb "gives" is "millions." The word "charities" is the indirect object. It completes the action of the verb.

> Erika **cooked everyone pancakes**. (Cooked pancakes *for whom?*)
> (verb)(indirect object)(direct object)

"Everyone" is the indirect object. It tells for whom Erika cooked the pancakes.

> Meredith **called** her **husband** a **shuttle**. (Called a shuttle *for whom?*)
> (verb)   (indirect object)(direct object)

Meredith doesn't think her husband *is* a shuttle. "Husband" is the indirect object. She arranged to have a shuttle to pick him up.

TIP: You can't have an indirect object if there is no direct object.

Object Complements

A complement completes. An **object complement** completes the meaning of a direct object of a verb. Adjectives, nouns, noun phrases, prepositional phrases, pronouns, and verb phrases can be object complements.

> Little Alex **made Drew his hero**.
> (verb) (direct object) (object complement)

The noun "hero" complements the direct object "Drew."

> Horrified, the nutritionist **watched** his **client crunching on pork rinds**.
> (verb)   (direct object)   (object complement)

"Crunching on pork rinds" complements the direct object "client."

> People **called Mr. Rogers "everyone's favorite neighbor."**
> (verb) (direct object)   (object complement)

The phrase "everyone's favorite neighbor" complements the direct object, Mr. Rogers.

Bob **brought** his world-famous "Bob's Own" salad dressing. (*Not,* **brang**—see page 203.)

Objects of Prepositions *(See prepositional phrases, page 145.)*
Objects of prepositions can be nouns or pronouns and their modifiers.

past the **dugout**
(preposition)(object—noun)

without her
(preposition)(object—pronoun)

ONOMATOPOEIA

9 CHICKWEED LANE by Brooke McEldowney

Decked out as Onomatopoeia Boy, Amos spews "words that reflect their meaning in their sound." Forming words by imitating sounds is called **onomatopoeia** (on uh maht´ uh pee´ uh.)

And how did Edda become Sesquipedalia Girl? By using extra-long words (*sesqui-*, one-and-a half," + *ped*, "foot"). Our advice? Eschew sesquipedalianism—avoid using words that are a foot-and-a-half long!

Thanks to onomatopoeia, words can help readers "hear" sounds:

babble	cuckoo	**Biff! Bam! Pow!**
hiss	screech	**boom**
pop	sizzle	**whippoorwill**

OXYMORONS

When two contradictory words are paired, they form an **oxymoron**. The word comes from two Greek word opposites, *oxy* ("sharp") + *moros* ("dull").

Here's a sampling of oxymorons:

alone together	awfully good	cruel kindness
diet ice cream	exact estimate	found missing
genuine imitation	jumbo shrimp	make haste slowly
near miss	organized chaos	same difference

Save oxymorons for emphasis, humor, or other special effects.

Ad: **Tuxedos**, $49.99. (*Not,* **Tuxedo's** or **Tuxedos'**—see page 135.)

DRABBLE by Kevin Fagan

P

PARENTHESES *(See also appositives, page 33, and relative pronouns, page 154.)*

Parentheses ( ) give the reader information that is helpful but not essential: The sentence would make sense without the words inside the parentheses.

> Special percussion instruments (slide whistle, duck quacker, and ratchet) make Copland's "Pops Hoedown" exciting.

Use parentheses:

▶ For interjecting a comment.
When a parenthetical statement falls inside another sentence, don't capitalize the first word or use a period inside the parentheses.

> Tyra Banks (she was a million-dollar model) also acts.

When a parenthetical question falls inside another sentence, don't capitalize the first word. But do use a question mark inside the parentheses.

> Ms. Fussbudget (isn't that a perfect name?) frets incessantly.

TIP: People who keep interrupting you to talk about themselves are irritating. Likewise, overuse of parentheses can irritate and confuse your reader:

> Bruno called (did I mention we're engaged?) to tell me that his friends (Henry, Thorvald, and Samantha) are coming for dinner (Bruno has a lot of nerve!).

Rudolph was different **from** the other reindeer. (*Not,* **than**—see page 72.)

▶ For adding a sentence as an aside.
When a parenthetical statement or question stands alone, do capitalize the first word and use end punctuation.

> We didn't finish the project today. (We did win the office Klondike tournament.)

> My blind date was a dud. (Who likes garlic breath?)

▶ To add omitted information.

> *Cold Mountain* (Charles Frazier) received rave reviews.

▶ For adding specific information.

> The remaining Beatles (Paul McCartney, Ringo Starr, and George Harrison) staged a reunion after John Lennon's death.

The parentheses set the list apart from the sentence. You could also use dashes. Presenting the list with commas instead of parentheses or dashes would be confusing because commas would be needed to separate the three musicians' names and after "Beatles." *(See dashes, page 66.)*

▶ For citing references within text in scholarly journals and academic papers. Some graduate schools follow the *Publication Manual of the American Psychological Association,* called the *APA Manual.* Using APA format, a quote that is a new reference must be followed with the author, date, and page.

> Ice-T said, "It's not a Warner Brothers fight; it's my fight" (Reston, 1992, 16).

> " . . . and the smallness of a research setting" (Jenson and Jankowski, 1991, 55).

Such cited references are an exception to the "period inside quotation marks" rule.

Many beginning university composition courses rely on the *Modern Language Association Handbook for Writers,* called the *MLA Handbook,* for citation format.

Choose one style manual and be consistent. *(For other recommended books, see More Grammar Resources, page 210.)*

Mama says, "Always wear clean **underwear**. " (*Not,* **underware**—see page 87,)

PARTS OF SPEECH

For a quick review of parts of speech, see the "Nitty-Gritty Grammar Refresher" (*page 7*). Or, turn to these specific listings: adjectives (*page 14*), adverbs (*page 17*), conjunctions (*page 61*), interjections (*page 102*), nouns (*page 118*), prepositions (*page 143*), pronouns (*page 147*), and verbs (*page 189*).

PASSED, PAST

"Passed" is the past tense of "to pass." It means "moved by."

> We **passed** the thatched cottages of Devon.

"Past" can function as an adverb, preposition, noun, or adjective. As an adverb, "past" means "beyond a point" or "by."

> The buffaloes thundered **past**.

As a preposition, "past" means "alongside" or "beyond."

> He drove **past** the house.
> (*preposition*)

"Past" can also be a noun or an adjective, meaning "before now."

> That pie-in-the-face caper is all in the **past**.
> (*noun*)

> This **past** week Daisy made curtains out of her bedspread.
> (*adjective*)

Don't confuse "past" with "passed." Instead of "I **past** the sword-swallowing test," use the verb "passed."

PEAK, PEEK, PIQUE

These three homophones are all pronounced "peek."

The verb "to peak" means "to achieve the highest point or intensity." The noun "peak" means "point or top." The adjective "peak" means "at the highest level."

> Crystal's acting career **peaked** when she was fourteen.

> Renny reached the **peak** of Mt. Sneffles just before 2 P.M.

> Randy gave a **peak** performance in the Ironman.

Maya Lin **pored** over the blueprints. (*Not*, **poured**—see page 90.)

The verb "to peek" means "to peer, glance, or show quickly." The noun "peek" means "a quick sly glance."

Peek at Boston's past.

Give me a **peek** at your little black book.

The verb "to pique" means "to stir or irritate." The noun "pique" means "a resentful feeling."

This Presto Veggie Slicer—just $9.99—will **pique** your interest.

In a fit of **pique**, Cuddles rejected the poached salmon.

PERCENT, PERCENTAGE

Half this game is 90 percent mental.

—Yogi Berra

Percentages show rates or proportions. You can use either "percent" or "percentage" if no number comes before.

A high **percent** (or **percentage**) of sweepstakes finalists are Libras.

▶ When using a specific number, follow the numeral with either "percent" or "%."

That high jumper must have about **10 percent** (or **10%**) body fat.

▶ Make "percent," meaning "rate per hundred," one word. It has evolved from the Latin *per centum*, "by the hundred."

▶ Place the percent sign right after the numeral (no space): **3%, 100%**. Use the percent sign (%) only for mathematical, scientific, or technical writing; otherwise, spell out the word.

▶ Separate the numeral and the word "percent" with a space.

The top score was **98 percent**.

▶ Repeat the percent sign each time in listing two or more percentages.

This Internet start-up company is expected to grow from **40%–50%** next year. (Note the unspaced en dash.)

Interest rates of **5%, 6%**, and **7%** are available.

Tommy Lee **lets** Al keep the window open. (*Not,* **let's**—see page 109.)

▶ Use a numeral, not a word, whether you use "%" or "percent."

> Ad: Valentine underwear **25%** off

> Donations fell by **81 percent** after our treasurer went to jail. (Do not write "eighty-one percent.")

THE BIG E: Use a word, not a numeral, with "percent" at the beginning of a sentence.

> **Seventy-four percent** of the union workers voted to strike.

Singular and Plural Verbs with "Percent" or "Percentage" (See articles, page 35.)

When the article "the" appears before "percentage," use a singular verb.

> **The percentage** of Palm Pilot devotees is rising. (*It* is rising.)

When the article "a" appears before "percentage," the prepositional phrase that follows "a percentage" tells you whether to use a singular or plural verb.

> A high **percent** of the voting **population** ignores the debates. (*It* ignores.)

> A high **percentage** of savvy **investors** use Motley Fool information. (*They* use.)

> A small **percent** of the muddy **footprints** are Fluffy's. (*They* are.)

PERIODS (See incomplete sentences, page 99.)

A period (.) says, "Stop!" Periods are end marks of punctuation and do other jobs, too. You may have been taught to put two spaces after a period. With today's proportional fonts, put only one space after a period.

Use periods:

▶ At the end of all complete sentences that don't end in a question mark or an exclamation mark.

> Chicago's Shedd Aquarium looks out on Lake Michigan.

▶ At the end of many abbreviations.

> etc.   cf.
> Dr.   Mrs.

(Use no spaces for academic degrees, such as M.A., Ph.D.)

> The **Jetsons'** dinner was a flop. (*Not,* Jetson's—see page 136.)

▶ After initials in a name.

W. E. B. Du Bois   **Robert E. Lee**   **C. S. Lewis**

Use a space between initials. (Some sources recommend no space between initials, but the Grammar Patrol votes with *The Chicago Manual of Style* on this one: We space initials.)

▶ In Web site addresses.

dunk.net	**Amazon.com**	**fineonline.com**
m-w.com	**monster.com**	**grammarpa-**
trol.com		

▶ After numbers in a list.
The onset of winter brings migratory urges to the following groups:

1. Common loons
2. Monarch butterflies
3. Canadian geese
4. Snowbirds

DID YOU KNOW? A period never falls outside of quotation marks in American English. This is a typographical convention. *(See quotation marks, page 163.)*

Felix said, "Try my famous broccoli-cheese bread." (*Not,* bread".)

PERSON
Verbs and pronouns have "person": first, second, and third. "Person" can be singular or plural. *(For more about this topic, see the charts in pronouns, page 148, and verbs, page 199.)*

PHOTOGENIC, PHOTOGRAPHIC
The adjective "photogenic" means "looks good in photos" (a **photogenic** baby). The adjective "photographic " means "used in photography" (**photographic** equipment) or "like a photograph in accuracy and detail" (a **photographic** memory).

PHRASALS
Have you ever noticed how some words always work together, like pair skaters? In Grammarspeak, these paired words are called **phrasals**. There are phrasal adjectives, phrasal prepositions, and phrasal verbs.

Sarah and Jim's **twins** were angels for Halloween. (*Not,* **two twins**—see page 169.)

Phrasal Adjectives (*See compound adjectives, page 14, and hyphens, page 91.*)
A **phrasal adjective** is any compound adjective or phrase used to modify a noun.

> **pet-loaded** SUV

> man **in the street**

> **Drooling into his dish,** the dog snarfed down the filet mignon.

Phrasal Prepositions

A **phrasal preposition** contains more than one word. Here are examples:

as to	by way of
except for	in lieu of
up to	with the exception of

TIP: In informal writing and speech, you can replace many phrasal prepositions with a simpler word. Use "instead" for "in lieu of." Use "about" for "with regard to."

Phrasal Verbs (*See among, between, page 27, and compare to, compare with, page 57.*)

CALVIN AND HOBBES by Bill Watterson

Phrasal verbs take specific prepositions, such as *abstain from, aim for, approve of, consist of, contingent upon,* and *lighten up.*

How are you? I'm **well.** (*Not, good*—see page 19.)

Some phrasal verbs can only take one specific preposition, while others can take two or more. Each combination creates a different meaning:

> consist of
> compare with *or* compare to
> distinguish between, distinguish among, *or* distinguish from

"Annoyed" takes "by"; "feel annoyed" takes "with" or "at."

> Lavonne was **annoyed by** Wally's boorish behavior.

> I **feel annoyed with** my mechanic; my car *still* stalls.

"Hanker" takes "after" or "for."

> Lynn **hankers after** pollo asada and menudo.

> Silver-tipped cowboy boots are what Alf **hankered for**.

"Meddle" takes "in" or "with."

> Parents shouldn't **meddle in** their children's decisions.

> Don't **meddle with** Alvina until she's had her coffee.

Suppose, Supposed (to)

Right
We're **supposed to have** lunch with the Obergs on Saturday.

Wrong
We're **suppose to have** lunch with the Obergs on Saturday.

? Why? Use the past tense of "suppose" when an infinitive like "to have" follows: supposed to have. "Supposed to" is often mistakenly written and said as "suppose to."

Use, Used (to)

Right
Louisa **used to** make gumbo every Saturday.

Wrong
Louisa **use to** make chicken gumbo every Saturday.

? Why? Use the past tense of the verb "to use" when an infinitive like "to make" follows: used to make. "Used to" is often mistakenly written and said as "use to."

Whose sneakers are these? (*Not,* **Who's**—see page 149.)

TIP: The forms of some words change, depending on the jobs they do in sentences. Using this chart, you know that you go to a **workout** to **work out**.

Noun	Verb	Adjective
carry-on	carry on	carry-on
drive-in	drive in	drive-in
follow-up	follow up	follow-up
grownup *or* grown-up	grow up	grown-up
mix-up	mix up	mixed-up
pickup	pick up	pickup
workout	work out	———

PHRASES

A phrase is a group of related words without a subject and a predicate. Phrases are never complete sentences. Phrases can be noun phrases, prepositional phrases, infinitive phrases, gerund phrases, and participial phrases.

> a mahogany grand piano (noun phrase)
> beside the swimming pool (prepositional phrase)
> to dance the light fantastic (infinitive phrase)
> watching basketball star Kevin Garnett (gerund phrase)
> glued to his cell phone (participial phrase)

PLURALS (*See consonants, vowels, page 64.*)

DRABBLE by Kevin Fagan

"Plural" means "more than one." Know the rules for making singular nouns plural.

"Dang! I just **sat** on my glasses!" (*Not*, **set**—see page 195.)

Making Singular Words Plural

▶ For most nouns, including those ending in a vowel followed by a **y**, simply add **s**.

kite/kites	pachyderm/pachyderms
lei/leis	monkey/monkeys
toy/toys	attorney/attorneys

▶ For words ending in **ch, s, sh, ss, x,** and **z**, add **es**.

peach/peaches	gas/gases
eyelash/eyelashes	kiss/kisses
box/boxes	one buzz/many buzzes

▶ If a word ends in **y** with a consonant before it, change the **y** to **i** and add **es**.

lady/ladies   sky/skies   story/stories

▶ If a word ends in **f** or **fe**, change the **f** or **fe** to **v** and add **es**.

half/halves   wolf/wolves   life/lives

THE BIG E: Not all nouns ending in **f** drop the **f** and add **ves**. Exceptions include che**fs**, goo**fs**, handkerchie**fs**, ree**fs**, roo**fs**, and staf**fs**.

▶ With most words ending in **o**, add **es**.

tomato/tomatoes   potato/potatoes   hero/heroes

THE BIG E: True to form, this rule has exceptions. "Ditto" becomes "ditto**s**." "Memo" becomes "memo**s**." The plural of "zero" is "zero**s**" or "zero**es**." Likewise, "hobo" can be "hobo**s**" or "hobo**es**."

▶ For musical words ending in **o**, just add **s**.

piccolo/piccolos   cello/cellos   alto/altos

Philip loves the **principle** of quality writing. (*Not*, **principal**—see page 90.)

Some plurals don't follow these rules:

Singular	Plural
cupful	cupfuls *or* cupsful
Grammy	Grammys *or* Grammies
hoof	hooves *or* hoofs
Kennedy	Kennedys
mouse	mice (for the rodent); mice *or* mouses (for the computer mouse)
treasury	treasuries (*but* "treasurys" for government securities)
thank-you	thank-yous (the notes)

Plurals with Contractions

To create plurals of contractions, simply add **s** to the contractions. In a *Beetle Bailey* cartoon by Mort Walker, General Halftrack shouts at Beetle, "No ifs, ands, or buts!" Beetle retorts, "How about some can'**ts**, won'**ts**, or don'**ts**?"

Plurals and Incorrect Apostrophes (*See apostrophes, page 30, and possessives, page 137.*)

Don't use apostrophes to create plurals. Apostrophes show possession.

 Right
Plurals: Use No Apostrophes

 Wrong
These Apostrophes Don't Belong

Employe**es** Only	Employe**'s** Only
Empty can**s** here	Empty can**'s** here
Bouquet**s**, $5.00	Bouquet**'s**, $5.00
Open Weekend**s**	Open Weekend**'s**

 Right
Jane sewed Tarzan's leopard suit**s**.

 Wrong
Jane sewed Tarzan's leopard suit**'s**.

? **Why?** "Suits" is plural, not possessive. No apostrophe is needed.

Jerry golfs **well**. (*Not,* good—see page 19.)

Plurals of Proper Nouns

Many people think that plurals of proper nouns need an apostrophe before the *s*, for example, Coke**'s**, Chevy**'s**, or Democrat**'s**. That's not so. Just write Coke**s**, Chevy**s**, and Democrat**s**. What's wrong on this invitation?

To the Parker**'s**

The card was meant for all the Parkers, not just one Parker. Make this a simple plural. Use no possessive apostrophe.

To the Parker**s**

If something belongs to the Parkers, put the possessive apostrophe after the *s* that makes "Parker" plural. (*See possessives, page 137.*)

the Parker**s'** plastic cow collection

Plurals of Names Ending in *s* (See possessives, page 137.)

If a proper noun ends in *s*, add *es* to make it plural.

The Haas**es** gathered in Chicago for a reunion.

Plurals of Compound Nouns

Some words add *s* to the most important word to make it plural.

Singular	Plural
attorney general	attorney**s** general (*not* attorney generals)
Chamber of Commerce	Chamber**s** of Commerce (*not* Chamber of Commerces)
chief-of-staff	chief**s**-of-staff (*not* chief-of-staffs)
commander in chief (no hyphens)	commander**s** in chief
mother-in-law	mother**s**-in-law (*not* mother-in-laws)
passerby	passer**s**by (*not* passerbys)
right-of-way	right**s**-of-way (*not* right-of-ways)
runner-up	runner**s**-up (*not* runner-ups)

Use a current dictionary to check noun plurals.

Ashford outperformed his **peers**. (*Not*, **piers**—see page 89.)

THE BIG E: There are some times, very rare, when an apostrophe helps readers to understand that a word is plural. "Do," for example, can be written "do's" in the plural (as in "do's and don'ts"). But because the meaning was clear, word maven Theodore Bernstein titled one of his books *Dos, Don'ts and Maybes of English Usage*. *(See apostrophes, page 30.)*

POSSESSIVES *(See pronouns as possessives, page 149.)*

How handy, alphabetically speaking, that the topic of **possessives** follows **plurals**. Remember, plurals show more than one. Possessives use apostrophes to show ownership.

Here's how to make words possessive.

Making Singular Words Possessive

▶ If a word, name, acronym, or initialism is singular, just add **'s**.

> the violin's strings   my teddy bear's tutu
>
> Skyla's Babysitting Service   Eudora Welty's writing
>
> Citigroup's president   NASA's next launch.
>
> The CEO's battered pickup truck attests to his frugality.

▶ With most singular nouns ending in **s**, add **'s**.

> kiss's imprint   grass's dead spots   bus's exhaust
>
> Four hundred children went on Mother Jones's march.
>
> Don Imus's ranch is for children with cancer.

THE BIG E: When a singular name that ends in **s** is followed by a word beginning with **s**, it's okay to use the apostrophe only (too many **s** sounds):

> Charles' sundae   Glynnis' sarcasm

▶ With religious or historical names of two or more syllables ending in **s**, just use an apostrophe after the **s**.

> Ulysses' journey   Moses' vision
>
> Jesus' disciples   (*But*, Zeus's thunderbolt,
>   because "Zeus" is one syllable.)

The peacocks preened **themselves**. (*Not*, **theirselves**—see page 151.)

DID YOU KNOW? To show joint ownership, add 's to the last word only. For individual ownership, add 's to each word.

Pierce and Jasmine's romance fizzled.

Leander's and Zilphy's bathing outfits matched.

Making Plural Words Possessive

▶ Some plural nouns don't end in *s*. Just add 's to make such words possessive.

Plural	Plural Possessive
children	children's swim floats
oxen	oxen's yokes
women	women's weight training

▶ To make plural nouns ending in *s* possessive, add an apostrophe after the *s*.

roller coasters	roller coasters' dips and turns
suitcases	suitcases' tags
eclairs	eclairs' custard filling

How does possession work with names? Let's say that the Owenses have bought a yacht. The name "Owens" has already been made plural with **es**: Owens**es**. Just add an apostrophe at the end: the Owenses' yacht.

The Owenses' yacht sailed into Boston Harbor.

Don and Fred sell Imus Brothers' Coffee.

TIP: With nouns ending in *s*, don't confuse the singular possessive with the plural possessive.

Tom Hanks's role in *Cast Away*
(*singular possessive*)

> *but*

the Coombses' new house
(*plural possessive*)

And never write "Charles Dicken's *Christmas Carol*." (That would mean "*A Christmas Carol* by Charles Dicken"! It should be "Charles Dickens's *Christmas Carol*.")

Where's the prom? (*Not,* Where's the prom **at**?—see page 146.)

Placing the Possessive Apostrophe

Many people simply guess about where to place apostrophes to show possession. Instead of the singular possessive "Bill Nye**'s** Tornado Model of Science," they incorrectly write "Bill Nye**s'** Tornado Model of Science." For the plural possessive "the Green Bay Packers**'** defense," they incorrectly write "the Green Bay Packer**'s** defense."

If placing the possessive apostrophe poses problems for you, take a look at these three methods.

Method One: The Two-Step Tango

1. Decide if the word is singular or plural.

     singular: helicopter   **plural: helicopters**

2. Add the mark of possession at the end of the word.

     singular: helicopter's flight   **plural: helicopters' flights**

Method Two: Draw an Arrow

Miss Hoezel, a wonderful eighth-grade English teacher, taught the arrow method for making words possessive.

1. Decide if the word is singular or plural, then draw a line under it.

     one <u>piglet</u> curly tail   ten <u>piglets</u> curly tails

2. Where the line ends, draw an "up" arrow.

     one <u>piglet</u> curly tail   ten <u>piglets</u> curly tails

3. Make an apostrophe at the tip of the arrow! (Add **s** to singular words.)

     one <u>piglet</u>'s curly tail   ten <u>piglets</u>' curly tails

Method Three: Say "of the" for Ownership

Switch the words around and say "of the" with the noun you want to make possessive. The apostrophe goes at the end of the noun that follows "of the."

Singular Nouns

     Dog: Make "the bowl **of the** dog" "the dog**'s** bowl."

     Superstar: Make "the trophies **of the** superstar" "the superstar**'s** trophies."

To **us** lab nerds, rats are vital. (*Not,* **we** lab nerds—see page 149.)

Plural Nouns

Dogs: Make "the bowls **of the** dogs" "the dogs' bowls."

Superstars: Make "the trophies **of the** superstars" "the superstars' trophies."

PREDICATE *(See sentences, page 174, and subject, page 183.)*

A sentence has two main parts: a **subject** and a **predicate**. The subject tells who or what a sentence or clause is about. The predicate is the verb, plus any other words linked to the verb (direct objects, adverbs, adjectives). It helps to know that the word "predicate" comes from Latin and means "what is said about what comes before." The predicate often describes what the subject of a sentence is doing. Predicates can be:

▶ Simple (one word: a verb).

> The teen **triumphed**.
> *(simple predicate)*

▶ Complete (a verb plus its objects and modifiers).

> Kristen **kicked the winning goal**.
> *(complete predicate)*

▶ Compound (two or more verbs or verb phrases and their modifiers).

> Esmerelda **sells makeup on the Internet and hosts a talk show**.
> *(compound predicate)*

PREDICATE ADJECTIVES *(See linking verbs, page 196.)*

Adjectives modify, so think of a **predicate adjective** as one that modifies the subject of a sentence. Joined to the subject by a linking verb, words in the predicate complete the meaning of the subject. Linking verbs include *be* (*am, is, are, was, were* . . .), *become, seem, appear, feel, look, taste, smell,* and *sound.*

> Dracula's **fangs looked creepy** at night.
> *(subject) (linking verb) (predicate adjective)*
> (The adjective "creepy" complements the subject "fangs.")

> To Nathan, **liver tastes yucky**.
> *(subject) (linking verb) (predicate adjective)*
> (The adjective "yucky" complements the subject "liver.")

Eight Sabots sailed in today's race. (*Not*, 8 Sabots—see page 121.)

140

Engineers **are analytical**.
(linking verb) (predicate adjective)
(The adjective "analytical" complements the subject "engineers.")

PREDICATE NOUNS *(See linking verbs, page 196, and subject-verb agreement, page 26.)*

Predicate nouns are single words or groups of words in the predicate that relate to the subject of a sentence. Like predicate adjectives, predicate nouns are joined to the subject by linking verbs.

Joel has become a Nature Conservancy board **member**.
(subject) (linking verb)   (predicate noun)

Whales are mammals.
(subject)(linking verb)(predicate noun)

PREFIXES, ROOTS, AND SUFFIXES *(See hyphens, page 91)*

Ready? Get out your decoder rings! Knowing the meanings of prefixes, roots, and suffixes is like knowing a secret code. When you're familiar with word parts drawn from Greek and Latin, or from German, Spanish, Arabic, French, and other languages, you can often figure out the meaning of difficult English words. (Etymology is the study of the origin and development of words.)

Prefixes are beginning word parts: *re-* (reapply), *dis-* (dishonest), *mid-* (mid-calf).

Roots are basic word elements: *hydro* (hydroelectric), *pod* (tripod), *graph* (autograph).

Suffixes are ending word parts: *-cracy* (democracy), *-less* (clueless), *-ment* (government).

Knowing the inside story on words can be magical. Astronauts, for instance, are "star sailors" (*astro* = "star" + *naut* = "sailor").

Prefixes

▶ *Pre-* means "before"; prefixes go before a root. Prehistoric animals lived before recorded history. Think pregame, preview, and preheat.

▶ *De-* means "from" or "away." "Defrost" means "to remove frost from." A dehumidifier takes water from the air.

▶ *Anti-* means "against." Think of your car's antifreeze.

I hope to see Gust soon. (*Not*, **Hopefully, I'll see**—see page 91.)

141

▶ *Meso-*, meaning "middle," can tip you off to the meaning of "mesosphere" (the middle layer of five layers of the earth's atmosphere).

THE BIG E: The prefix *in-* sometimes means "not," as in "inhospitable." But surprisingly, "flammable" and "inflammable" mean the same thing: "able to burn."

DID YOU KNOW? The prefix *bi-* means "two." Think "bicycle" or "biceps." *Bi-* can also mean "twice each" or "every two." Be sure you know if a "bimonthly" meeting means "twice a month" or "every other month." Why not label the meeting "twice a month" or "every other month" instead?

Hyphens with Prefixes *(See also hyphens, page 91.)*

▶ Only hyphenate words with prefixes, such as *non-, pre-,* and *un-* when what follows the prefix is capitalized: non-Italian, pre-Elvis, un-American, non-European.

▶ Capitalize prefixes only when they fall at the beginning of a sentence, when prefixes are part of a proper compound word, or when prefixes appear in a title.

Pre-prom jitters tax sweat glands. (beginning of sentence)

"Anti-Fashion Police Parade" (title)

▶ Put a hyphen after the prefix when prefixes suggest a span of time.

pre- and post-game shows

mid- to late 1980s

(Note the space after *pre-* and *mid-*. If "and post-" and "to late" were vacuumed out, these would read "pre-game shows" and "mid-1980s.")

Roots

Think of a root as the base of a word. *Rhino* means "nose." *Ceros* means "horn." A rhinoceros has a horn on its nose. *Aqua* and *hydr* mean "water." Think of "aquarium" and "fire hydrant." *Ped* and *pod* mean "foot." Think of "pedestrian" and "tripod."

The roots *graph* and *gram* mean "write, written." Combine *graph* and *gram* with *auto-* ("self"), *photo-* ("light"), or *tele-* ("far") and you get "autograph" ("self-written"—your signature), "photograph" ("written with light"), or "telegram" ("written from afar").

You can decode harder words, too. The root *arthr* means "joint." The

---

Take that jalopy to the junkyard. (*Not,* **Bring**—see page 42.)

suffix *-itis* means "inflammation." "Arthritis" is inflammation of the joint. "Rhinitis" is inflammation of the nose or its membranes. Add the prefix *acro-* ("high, top") to the root *phobia* ("fear of"), and you get "acrophobia" ("fear of heights").

David's **acrophobia** made him clutch Jane in the glass elevator.

Suffixes

Suffixes are word endings. Simple suffixes include *-ed, -ing,* and *-ly.* The suffix *-ant* means "a person or thing that does."

An applicant applies.

A contestant competes in a contest.

A lubricant, like WD-40, lubricates.

Other suffixes include *-orama* ("view") and *-fer* ("bear, carry"). Combined with *pan-* ("all"), or *trans-* ("across"), you get "panorama" and "transfer."

To learn more about roots, prefixes, and suffixes, check an up-to-date dictionary or the Internet. *(Also see More Grammar Resources, page 210).*

PREPOSITIONS *(See phrasal prepositions, page 131.)*

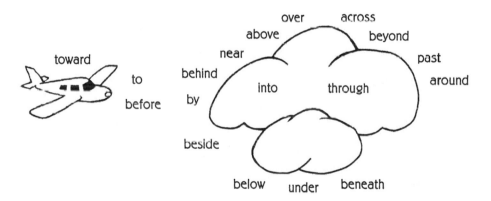

Prepositions (*pre-* + "position") take a *position before* a noun or pronoun. They can show position or time, or they can indicate a comparison or connection. (Prepositions can also show relationships or manner.)

The Insta-Cam caught **both** of you. (*Not,* **the both**—see page 41.)

Use the "plane and cloud" trick on page 143 to help you remember most prepositions. The plane can fly **near** the cloud, **by** the cloud, **above** the cloud, **into** the cloud, **through** the cloud, **under** the cloud, **over** the cloud . . .

Position Prepositions

about	below	inside	through
above	beneath	into	throughout
across	beside	near	to
against	between	off	toward
along	beyond	on	under
amid	by	onto	underneath
among	down	out	up
around	for	outside	upon
at	from	over	within
behind	in	past	without

These are heady good times for Mike Piazza, the Mets' star catcher.

Karrie Webb's golf ball sailed **over** the sand trap.

Catherine's *Counterpanes* exhibit hung **on** the gallery wall.

Some prepositions, such as "beside" and "toward," have an **s** form: "besides" and "towards." The preposition "toward" is used more often in American English and "towards" in British English. *(See beside, besides, page 40.)*

Time Prepositions

about	after	before
during	since	until

The five-meter snail race lasted **about** three hours.

After his military career, Dwight Eisenhower became president.

Comparison Prepositions *(See among, between, page 27, and as, like, page 37.)*

as	like
unlike	between

Like Houdini, David Copperfield is a great escape artist.

Unlike Aunt Blanche, Ben had no idea how to use jumper cables.

Bucky and Satchel often **clash**. (*Not,* **clashes**—see page 183.)

Connector Prepositions

about	except	for	from
of	to	with	

Kirsten served chicken breast dripping **with** avocado sauce.

Everyone fits in the van **except** Sugar, our Great Dane.

Prepositional Phrases

A **prepositional phrase** combines a preposition with one or more nouns or pronouns. The nouns or pronouns that follow prepositions are called **objects of prepositions**.

<u>underneath</u> his <u>cloak</u>
(preposition) *(object—noun)*

<u>to</u> <u>Manny, Moe,</u> and <u>Jack</u>
(preposition) *(object—nouns)*

<u>for</u> <u>them</u>
(preposition) (object—pronoun)

<u>like</u> <u>him</u> and <u>her</u>
(preposition) (object—pronouns)

Remember! Prepositions take the objective form of pronouns. *(See Chart 2, page 148.)*

To End or Not to End?

This is the sort of English up with which I will not put.

—Winston Churchill

ZITS by Jerry Scott and Jim Borgman

There used to be a firm rule about never ending a sentence with a preposition. That rule has relaxed. Sentences rearranged to avoid a preposition at the end can sound huffy and overblown, as in Churchill's spoof above.

I can't eat marinated herring **anymore**. (*Not*, **no more**—see page 116.)

In informal speech and writing, use common sense. These sentences are fine:

Who did Minnie Driver study **with**?

Which state are you **from**?

Which bucket should I haul the oysters **in**?

In formal speech and writing, it's still best to avoid ending a sentence with a preposition.

With whom did you study elocution?

From which satellite did the signal originate?

In which garage should Chauncy park the Stutz Bearcat?

The Grammar Patrol does take a stand against these two constructions:

Where's it **at**? (Say, "Where is it?")

Where is he going **to**? (Say, "Where is he going?")

Prepositions with Phrasals (*See phrasal prepositions, page 131, and phrasal verbs, page 131.*)

MOMMA by Mell Lazarus

Some prepositions are made up of several words. (In Grammarspeak, they're called "phrasal prepositions.")

in the middle of   **for the purpose of**

Some verbs, called phrasal verbs, are made up of a verb and a specific preposition.

buckle up   **turn in**

Lend me your razor, please. (*Not*, loan—see page 109.)

146

PREVENTIVE, PREVENTATIVE

"Preventive" can be an adjective meaning "serving to prevent" or a noun meaning "an agent to prevent disease" or "a measure for preventing something." Dictionaries do recognize the alternative "preventative," but "preventive" is far more common.

Frieda uses duct tape as a wrinkle **preventive**.

PRONOUNS *(For pronouns and linking verbs, see subject complements, page 184.)*

B.C. by Johnny Hart

A NOUN THAT HAS GIVEN UP ITS AMATEUR STATUS.

Pronouns are noun substitutes. In sentences, a pronoun does the same job as the noun it replaces.

> **Stewart Pinkerton** is the deputy managing editor of *Forbes*.
> *(noun)*

> **He** is the deputy managing editor of *Forbes*.
> *(pronoun)*

Pronouns have number, person, and case.

> **Number:** singular or plural
> **Person:** first, second, or third
> **Case:** subjective (in Grammarspeak, "nominative"), objective, or possessive

Pronouns have different forms, depending on the nouns they replace.

Pronouns as Subjects

Subjective pronouns act as **subjects**. They substitute for nouns that are subjects of clauses or complete sentences.

Rick's an **eminent** oceanographer. (*Not*, **imminent**—see page 76.)

Subjective Pronouns (Chart 1)

Person	Singular	Plural
First	I	we
Second	you	you
Third	he, she, it (who, whoever)	they

If a pronoun acts as a subject, use the subjective forms found in Chart 1.

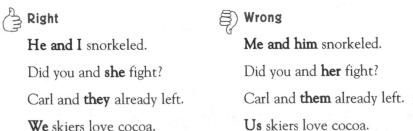

👍 Right	👎 Wrong
He and I snorkeled.	**Me and him** snorkeled.
Did you and **she** fight?	Did you and **her** fight?
Carl and **they** already left.	Carl and **them** already left.
We skiers love cocoa.	**Us** skiers love cocoa.
Pedro and **she** are engaged.	**Her** and Pedro are engaged.

TIP: Still puzzled? Vaccuum out extra words, leaving only the pronoun. Say, "**I** snorkeled," *not* "**Me** snorkled."

Pronouns as Objects

Objective pronouns act as **objects**. They substitute for nouns that are the objects of verbs or prepositions.

Objective Pronouns (Chart 2)

Person	Singular	Plural
First	me	us
Second	you	you
Third	him, her, it (whom, whomever)	them

If a pronoun acts as an object of a verb or preposition, use the objective forms found in Chart 2.

Marvin plowed **farther** than Donnie. (*Not,* **further**—see page 78.)

Object of a Verb

 Right **Wrong**

Photograph Elmo and **me**.   Photograph Elmo and **I**.

Take Michael or **her**.   Take Michael or **she**.

Call Dr. Joy and **him**.   Call Dr. Joy and **he**.

TIP: Again, vacuum out extra words. Say, "Photograph **me**," *not* "Photograph **I**."

Object of a Preposition

 Right **Wrong**

It's up to **us** point guards.   It's up to **we** point guards.

Between you and **me** . . .   Between you and **I** . . .

This candy's for **them** and Harry.   This candy's for **they** and Harry.

DID YOU KNOW? Use the objective form if the pronoun is the object of an infinitive:

to introduce him   **to woo her**   **to marry them**

Pronouns as Possessives
Possessive pronouns show **possession**.

Possessive Pronouns (Chart 3)

Person	Singular	Plural
First	my, mine	our, ours
Second	your, yours	your, yours
Third	his, her, hers, its (whose)	their, theirs (whose)

To show ownership, use the possessive pronoun forms in Chart 3. Notice how some forms of possessive pronouns stay the same.

This is his Frisbee.   **This Frisbee is his.**

Jan ate **fewer** shrimp than Keith. (*Not*, less—see page 78.)

Other pronouns change form, depending on how they're used in a sentence.

These are my bagels.	These bagels are mine.
These are her pliers.	These pliers are hers.
You ate our radishes!	Those radishes were ours.
Is that your scooter?	That scooter is yours.
It's their secret recipe.	The secret recipe is theirs.

TIP: Don't confuse the possessive pronoun "its" with the contraction "it's." Possessive **its** never spl**its**.

"Viagra and **Its** Fiscal Impact"
> *not*

"Viagra and **It's** Fiscal Impact"

Possessive Pronouns and Gerunds *(See verbs, page 191.)*
Remember gerunds? They're the ***ing*** forms of verbs, which act as nouns. A good rule of thumb has been to use a possessive pronoun before a gerund. Nowadays, not everybody follows this rule. But the Grammar Patrol still prefers to use the possessive forms of pronouns with gerunds.

Janet appreciated **his calling** home. (*Not,* **him calling**.)

Mom hated the thought of **their leaving** the nest. (*Not,* **them leaving**.)

The boss okayed **our going** to Sweden. (*Not,* **us going**.)

"Self"-Ending Pronouns
"Self"-ending pronouns end in ***self*** or ***selves*** and must refer to someone or something in the same clause or sentence. (In Grammarspeak, "self"-ending pronouns are called "reflexives" or "reflexive pronouns.")

I pulled the taffy **myself**.

Sandra mixed the glazes **herself**.

Dr. Powell **pored** over the day's reports. (*Not,* **poured**—see page 90.)

Pronouns That End in "Self" (Chart 4)

Person	Singular	Plural
First	myself	ourselves
Second	yourself	yourselves
Third	himself, herself, itself (*never* hisself)	themselves (*never* themself or theirselves)

Pronouns ending in **self** can also emphasize:

> **Troy Aikman himself** helps football stars find sponsors.

Common "Self"-Ending Pronoun Bloopers
People often use "self"-ending pronouns where they don't belong:

> Annie and **I** are in charge of the Dunk-the-Teacher Booth.
>> *not*
> Annie and **myself** are in charge of the Dunk-the-Teacher Booth.

Unless a "self"-ending pronoun refers to someone or something in the same clause or sentence, use a subjective or objective pronoun instead.

 Right
Hand your boarding passes to **me**.

 Wrong
Hand your boarding passes to **myself**.

? **Why?** This airline employee needs to use the objective pronoun "me," the object of the preposition "to." "Myself" doesn't refer to anything in the sentence.

Indefinite Pronouns
Indefinite pronouns substitute for nouns that refer in general to people, places, things, ideas, and qualities. Some indefinite pronouns always take singular verbs. Others always take plural verbs. Some indefinite pronouns can be singular or plural, depending on the words that follow. Substitute "he" or "she" or other pronouns to test the verb form you choose.

As I said, eggnog's not exactly lowfat. (*Not*, Like—see page 37.)

9 CHICKWEED LANE by Brooke McEldowney

  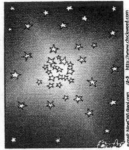 

Singular Indefinite Pronouns

Use a singular verb with these pronouns: *anybody, anyone, each, either, every, everybody, everyone, neither, nobody, no one, nothing, one.*

> **Everyone knows** young William is Prince Charming. (*He* or *she* knows young William is Prince Charming.)

> **Nobody likes** tired lettuce. (*He* or *she* likes tired lettuce.)

Plural Indefinite Pronouns

Use a plural verb with these pronouns: *both, few, many, several.*

> **Many are** mystery buffs. (*They* are mystery buffs.)

> **Few are** true sleuths. (*They* are true sleuths.)

Singular or Plural Indefinite Pronouns

Memorize these five versatile pronouns: *all, any, most, some* and the prickly *none.* These indefinite pronouns can be singular if singular words follow them, or plural, if plural words follow them:

All

> **All** of the red licorice **has** vanished.
> ("Licorice" is singular. *It* has vanished.)

> **All** of those lava lamps **are** hideous.
> ("Lamps" is plural. *They* are hideous.)

"Breaking the Code was **stupendous!"** (*Not,* stupendous"! —see page 165.)

Any

> If **any** of Stephanie's birthday cake **is missing**, you're in trouble.
> ("Cake" is singular. *It* is missing.)

> **Any** of the wedding guests **could protest** the match.
> ("Guests" is plural. *They* could protest.)

Most

> **Most** of the trail **is** open.
> ("Trail" is singular. *It* is open.)

> **Most** of the rides **are** tame.
> ("Rides" is plural. *They* are tame.)

Some

> **Some** of the shipment **was damaged**.
> ("Shipment" is singular. *It* was damaged.)

> **Some** of the wilder fans **honk** horns.
> ("Fans" is plural. *They* honk.)

None

> **None** of the escargot paté **is** left.
> ("Paté" is singular. *Not any of it* is left.)

"None" is singular when it means "not any of it" or "none of it."

> **None** of the jugglers **use** bowling balls.
> ("Jugglers" is plural. *They* use bowling balls.)

When "none" means "not any" or "none of them," use a plural verb.

TIP: If by "none," you mean "not one," then say, "not one."

> **Not one** of the belly dancers wears polyester.

Even though belly dancers is plural, "not one" is singular. Use a singular verb. Say, "Not one **wears** polyester," *not* "Not one **wear** polyester."

The feisty clerk's nickname is **"Spitfire."** (*Not,* **"Spitfire".** —see page 165.)

Demonstrative Pronouns

Demonstrative pronouns demonstrate: They point out specific nouns. Demonstrative pronouns include *this, these, that,* and *those.*

> this stock option   these career decisions
>
> that cranberry bog   those swimsuits

Interrogative Pronouns

Interrogative pronouns ask questions: *what, which, who, whom,* and *whose.*

> **What** is calamari—squid or octopus?
>
> **Who** swiped my *Buena Vista Social Club* CD?
>
> **Whose** dirty socks are in my drawer?

Relative Pronouns *(See pronoun-antecedent agreement, page 25.)*

Relative pronouns show relationships: *that, what, which, who, whom,* and *whose.* These pronouns relate to a noun that appears earlier (an antecedent) in the sentence. Clauses that start with a relative pronoun serve as adjectives.

> The maniac **who called** was my boss.
>
> The kazoo concert, **which took place Saturday**, annoyed the neighbors.

That or Which?

The pronouns "that" and "which" are often confused. The pronoun you choose depends on the type of clause the pronoun introduces.

▸ Use "that" with essential clauses.
Use the pronoun "that" with essential clauses—those that give information essential to the sentence. "That" clauses have no commas. (In Grammarspeak, essential clauses are called "restrictive clauses.")

> The skunk **that dug under the fence** ate my parsley.
>
> *(essential clause)*

▸ Use "which" with nonessential clauses.
Use the pronoun "which" with nonessential clauses—those that contain information not needed for the sentence to make sense. "Which" clauses have commas. (In Grammarspeak, nonessential clauses are called "nonrestrictive clauses.")

> The musical *Lion King,* **which was first a movie,** starts Friday.
>
> *(nonessential clause)*

Potato chips are Ron's only **vice**. (*Not,* **vise**—see page 209.)

That or Who?

Officially, both "that" and "who" can refer to people. But since "that" can also refer to things, the Grammar Patrol recommends using "who" for people.

> Campers **who** skinny-dip should do so after dark.

> The tweezers **that** I always use have disappeared.

Who or Whom?

MOTHER GOOSE AND GRIMM by Mike Peters

Who—Always a Subject

Use "who" for the subject of a sentence or clause. *(See Chart 1, page 148.)* A verb follows the pronoun "who."

> **Who wants** some key lime pie?
> *(subject of sentence) (verb)*

> Joanne, **who planted** all the flowers, is an ace gardener.
> *(subject of clause) (verb)*

The "who" could trip you up in this example:

> Sidney asked about **who did** the driving.
> *(subject of clause) (verb)*

"Who" is the subject of the clause "who did the driving," not the object of the preposition "about." Instead, the whole clause—"who did the driving"—is the object of the preposition "about."

The herd of Holsteins **heads** for the barn. (*Not*, head—see page 51.)

Whom—Always an Object

Use "whom" as the object of a verb or a preposition. *(See Chart 2, page 148.)*

Nortel **hired whom**?
(verb) (direct object of a verb)

For whom does Tommy Hilfiger make clothes? All ages.
(preposition) (object of a preposition)

Tricks for Deciding on Who or Whom

With longer or more complex sentences, the "who or whom?" puzzle grows.

▶ Rearrange the sentence.

Felix was the man **whom** Oscar called.

Rearranged: **Oscar** called **whom**?
(subject) *(direct object)*

▶ Substitute a different pronoun for "who" or "whom."
Use "he, him" or "she, her" in place of "who, whom" to see which pronoun to use. (Like "who," "he" and "she" are subjects. Like "whom," "him" and "her" are objects.)

Lee called (**who** or **whom**) about the cruise? (whom)

Lee called (**she** or **her**) about the cruise? (her)

▶ Omit words to help you decide.
Leave out phrases like "he knows," "I believe," "she thinks," and "they say" to help you decide on "who" or "whom."

I'm studying Truman, (**who** or **whom**) I believe was president after Roosevelt.

I'm studying Truman, **who** [I believe] was president after Roosevelt.

MNEMONIC (MEMORY AID): "Hi**m**," "the**m**," and "who**m**" all end in **m**, and are all objective.

▶ Add implied words.
Implied words can help you choose the right pronoun (subjective or objective).

Sancho plays the bassoon better than **she** [does].

Steffi likes tennis better than **I** [do].

Steffi likes tennis better than [she likes] **me**.

I **can hardly** wait for graduation. (*Not*, **can't hardly**—see page 116.)

PRONUNCIATION

We're bombarded daily by mispronounced words. Take "nuclear." On TV and radio, we hear "noo´ **cue** ler" for the correct "noo´ **clee** er." There's a "clee," *not* a "cue" in "nuclear"!

Even the word "pronunciation" causes problems. There's a "nun," *not* a "noun" in this word. Say, "pro **nun**´ see ay´ shun," *not* "pro **noun**´ see ay´ shun." This mix-up happens because the word "pronounce" does have a "noun" sound.

We strongly recommend Charles Harrington Elster's books on pronunciation, particularly his *Big Book of Beastly Mispronunciations.*

Words can be funny when mispronounced. Some people call Marie **Callender's** pie shop Marie **Colander's.** (Handy for rinsing pie berries.) Here are other funny pronunciation bloopers. (Accented syllables are marked.)

Word	👍 Right	👎 Wrong
epitome	eh pih´ **tuh mee**	eh´ pih ~~tome~~ (rhymes with "Rome")
gnome	**nome**	~~guh~~ nome´
gnu	**noo**	~~guh~~ noo´
paradigm	par´ uh **dime** (*or* par´ uh **dim**)	pair´ uh ~~dih gum~~ *or* pair´ uh ~~dih jum~~

Some words are pronounced differently depending on their part of speech.

conflict noun (con´ flict): a clash, fighting
     verb (con flict´): to clash, to differ

tear noun (rhymes with "ear"): a drop of fluid from the eye
   noun (rhymes with "bear"): a rip
   verb (rhymes with "bear"): to rip

Some confusing words are spelled almost alike and can also cause mix-ups in speech. An announcer on a classical music station said, "Let this music of Mozart **envelope** you." (She meant "**envelop**.")

envelope noun (en´ veh lope): a flat, paper container

envelop verb (en veh´ lup): to enclose

A number of cruise passengers **overeat**. (*Not,* **overeats**—see page 36.)

157

These measurement words are often pronounced incorrectly:

height   Say, "hite" (*Not,* "hithe": "Height" does not end in ***th.***)

length   Say, "lengkth" (*Not,* "lenth": Give the ***g*** a tip of the hat.)

width   Say, "width" (*Not,* "with": Pronounce the ***d.***)

DRABBLE by Kevin Fagan

Even as Drabble reminds his sister about the hard **c** sound in "picture," Penny knows that baseball's Hideo Nomo is a "pitcher," not a "picture."

Check this list of words that are often mispronounced. (Accented syllables are marked.)

Word	👍 Right	👎 Wrong
accept	**ack** sept´	~~us~~ sept´
accessible	**ak** seh´ sih ble	~~us~~ seh´ sih ble
across	uh **cross**´	uh ~~crosst~~ (Don't end with ***t.***)
ask, asked	**ask, askt**	~~ax, axed,~~ *or* ~~ast~~
athlete	**ath**´ lete	a´ th~~uh~~ lete
camaraderie	com´ **mah** rah´ deh ree (five syllables)	~~com rah~~´ deh ree (*not* four syllables)
couldn't	**cood**´ **unt** (two syllables)	~~koont~~ (*not* one syllable)
centimeter	**sen**´ tih mee ter	~~sahn~~´ tih mee ter
consonant	con´ **seh nunt**	con´ ~~stuh~~ nunt *or* con´ ~~stuh nut~~
coup (deed or feat)	**koo**	~~coop~~ *or* ~~cue~~ (Don't say the ***p.***)

Tom removed the door from **its** frame. (*Not,* **it's**—see page 105.)

coupe (two-door car)	coop or koo pay´	~~eyoup~~
didn't	did´ unt	~~dint~~ (*not* one syllable)
dissect	dih sect´	~~die~~ sect´ *or* ~~die´~~ sect
effect	eh fect´	~~ee´~~ fect
eighty	ate´ ee (Say the *t*.)	~~aid´~~ ee
et cetera	et seh´ tuh ruh	~~eck~~ seh´ tuh ruh (There's no "eck" in et cetera.)
foliage	foe´ lee ij (three syllables)	~~foy´~~ lee ij *or* ~~foe´~~ lij (*not* two syllables)
forte (strong point)	fort (or, frequently, for´ tay)	for´ ~~teh~~ *or* for ~~tay´~~ (Don't emphasize the second syllable.)
grievous	gree´ **vus** (two syllables)	gree´ ~~vee~~ us (*not* three syllables)
important, importance	im por´ **tant**, im por´ **tense**	im por´ ~~dant~~, im por´ ~~dense~~
infuriate	in **fyur´** ee ate (four syllables)	in fyur´ ee ~~or~~ ate (*not* five syllables)
intact	in **tact´** (Say the end *t*.)	in ~~tack´~~
jewelry	joo´ **wul** ree	joo´ ~~luh~~ ree
library	lie´ **brair** ee	lie´ ~~bair~~ ee
mathematics	math´ **eh** mat´ icks	math ~~mat´~~ icks
mischievous	mis´ **chih vus** (three syllables; emphasize the first)	mis ~~chee´~~ ~~vee~~ us (*not* four syllables with emphasis on second)
picture	**pick´** ture	~~pitch´~~ er (Don't say "pitch.")
poinsettia	poyn seh´ **tee** uh (four syllables)	poyn ~~seh´~~ ~~tuh~~ (*not* three syllables) *or* ~~point~~ seh tuh (no *t* sound)
salmon	**saa´** muhn (as in "Sam," silent *l*)	~~sal´~~ muhn (Don't say the *l*.)

Meet me at the **ATM** on San Dieguito. (*Not*, **A.T.M.** —see page 14.)

short-lived	short-**lived** (long *i*)	short-~~lihved~~ (*not* short *i*)
similar	sih´ **muh** ler	sih´ ~~myuh~~ ler
strict	**strihkt** (say the hard *c* and *t*)	~~strick~~
template	tem´ **pliht**	tem´ ~~plate~~ *
verbiage	vir´ **bee** ij (three syllables)	~~ver´ bij~~ (*not* two syllables)
versus	**ver´ sus** (two syllables)	~~verse~~ (*not* one syllable)
vice versa	**vie´** seh ver´ seh	~~viee~~ ver´ seh

** Template: A few dictionaries now recognize the long **a** pronunciation of "-plate." We go with the majority that list only "tem´ pliht."*

PUN (*See figures of speech, page 79.*)

PUNCTUATION (*See individual marks of punctuation by name.*)

BABY BLUES by Rick Kirkman and Jerry Scott

Punctuation is a code to help readers ride smoothly through writing. Think of punctuation marks as traffic signals:

I love *For Better or for Worse*. (*Not*, "For Better or for Worse"—see page 103.)

. **Period = Stop Sign**
Come to a full stop. Then go on—no sliding through.

, **Comma = Flashing Yellow Light**
Slow down, look left and right, then continue.

; **Semicolon = Flashing Red Light**
Stop briefly; forge ahead.

: **Colon = Arrow or Road Sign**
Listen up! What follows explains or adds information.

( ) and — **Parentheses and Dashes = Detour**
Take a quick detour—then proceed.

Q

QUALIFIERS (See modifiers, page 114.)

Parent: "Did you pick up the dog poop, dear?"

Teen: "**Kind of, in a way, a little, sort of . . .**"

Qualifiers modify meaning. They are words or groups of words that limit or describe other words.

sometimes flirty	**rather plain**
quite snobbish	**a bit hairy**

Qualifiers are often vague, wishy-washy, nonspecific. Overusing qualifiers can weaken your writing, reducing clarity and sharpness of detail. Be "clear," *not* "**pretty** clear."

won in a very real sense	**pretty much over it**
sort of overdrawn	

QUESTION MARKS

A question mark (**?**) signals that a sentence asks a question. Put one space after a question mark at the end of a sentence. Do not follow a question mark with a period: Is that so**?** (*Not,* is that so**?.**)

Ad: Dogs **spayed** here. (*Not,* **spade**—see page 90.)

161

Direct Questions

Use a question mark in sentences that ask a direct question. The interrogative pronouns *who, what, which, where,* and *why* often indicate a question. So does the verb "do."

> **Who** ate all the Krispy Kremes?

> **Do** you watch *Jeopardy?*

Direct questions can fall within a larger sentence, especially when people are thinking something to themselves. When that happens, place the question mark right after the question itself. Don't use quotation marks.

> Was that a toupee on Dudley's head? pondered Wanda.

> Alicia wondered, **W**ould a toga be right for the costume party? (Note the capital *w* on "would," the start of the question itself.)

Indirect Questions

Sometimes a question is implied but not asked directly. Indirect questions often express inner thoughts. Because an indirect question is a statement, follow it with a period, not a question mark. Leave quotation marks off when the question is indirect.

> The question is whether lemon juice will enhance this perm mixture.

> Colleen wondered if her fruitcakes were done.

> The teacher asked if the dog ate my homework once again.

MNEMONIC (MEMORY AID): Indirect questions **state.** **State**ments end with periods.

Rhetorical Questions

Rhetorical questions are ones for which you don't expect answers. They take a question mark.

> How many hockey games can there be in one weekend?

> Is it any wonder that the seams burst?

TIP: Don't overuse rhetorical questions.

A Series of Questions

When several questions occur within one sentence, use question marks, but only capitalize the first word of the sentence.

The crooks' alibis didn't **jibe.** (*Not,* **jive**—see page 105.)

Who does Georgette think she is? queen? empress? ruler of the universe?

Questions and Quoted Words

If a question applies only to the quoted words, put the question mark inside the end quotation mark.

> "O Romeo, Romeo, wherefore art thou Romeo?" whispered Juliet.

DID YOU KNOW? By saying "wherefore," a distraught Juliet is not asking *where* Romeo is. She's asking *why* he is a Montague, her family's sworn enemy, and not someone whom she could marry.

Questions Within Questions

If a sentence not only asks a direct question but also ends in a word or phrase that includes a question mark, use only one question mark.

> Have you seen *Who Framed Roger Rabbit?* (*Not, Rabbit?!*)

Questions Inside Parentheses

When a question falls inside a parenthetical thought in a sentence, you don't capitalize the beginning of the question. Do put a question mark at the end of the question.

> We asked applicants to submit references (who wouldn't?) and a credit summary.

QUOTATION MARKS

ZITS by Jerry Scott and Jim Borgman

The cop **implied** Tilly was speeding. (*Not,* **inferred**—see page 99.)

Quotation marks (" ") have several jobs. Use them:

▶ To quote someone's exact words.

> "You are my own sweet lamb chop," said Irving.

▶ To enclose quotations.

> "Twas brillig and the slithy toves / Did gyre and gimble in the wabe . . ." ("Jabberwocky," Lewis Carroll)

▶ To enclose titles of shorter works. *(See italics, page 102, for longer works.)*

> **Short poems:** "Touch Me" (Stanley Kunitz)
> **Songs:** "Fly Away" (John Denver)
> **Stories:** "Three Billy Goats Gruff"
> **Short stories:** "Teaching Luther to Cook" (Bailey White, *Mama Makes Up Her Mind*)
> **Articles:** "Wallflowers in a Hot Market" (Bob Howard, *Los Angeles Times*)
> **Chapters of books:** "The House of Fear" (Robert Louis Stevenson, *Kidnapped*)
> **Short musical compositions:** "Adagio for Strings" (Samuel Barber)
> **Individual episodes of radio or TV shows:** "Radar's Report" (*M*A*S*H*)

▶ To set off individual words, phrases, or nicknames. (Nicknames, also called "sobriquets," sometimes appear in quotation marks.)

> Veteran golfer Tom Walters called Tiger Woods "supernatural," the best in the world.

> Gary Paulsen's "tame house dog" was half wolf.

> Jesse ("the Body") Ventura was elected governor of Minnesota.

If the nickname is used as a renamer (appositive), you don't need parentheses or quotation marks.

> Jimmy Durante, **the Schnoz**, was a comedy legend.

Oliver shifted into listening **mode**. (*Not,* **mood**—see page 114.)

When you substitute a nickname for a person's name, capitalize the nickname, but don't use quotation marks.

Satchmo was known for his trumpet solos and gravelly voice.

9 CHICKWEED LANE by Brooke McEldowney

Punctuation with Quotation Marks

Three inside-outside rules can help you punctuate with quotation marks.

1. Periods and commas *always* go inside quotation marks.

   Henry said, "A runaway bull ended our picnic." (*Not,* picnic".)

   The surfer pulled an "off the lip." (*Not,* lip".)

   Amy's airy office, "the treehouse," (*not,* treehouse",) was her refuge.

2. Colons and semicolons *always* go outside quotation marks.

   Morris Munon was "FTA": That's "failure to appear" in bounty-hunter lingo.

   —*Hot Six,* Janet Evanovich

   The island get away was billed as a "pleasure trip"; it was more like an endurance test.

3. Question marks, dashes, and exclamation points can go inside *or* outside. Where you put them depends on what you mean to say.

When ?, —, ! Go Inside

Put these marks (? , —, !) *inside* the quotation marks if they apply only to the quoted material.

      " . . .?"   " . . .—"   " . . .!"

My bulldog is so **photogenic.** (*Not,* **photographic**—see page 130.)

Question Mark Inside Quotation Marks

Put the question mark inside the end quotation mark when it only applies to the quoted material. Below, the question mark refers only to the song title. The sentence is a statement.

> Ted's favorite country song was "How Can I Heal My Boomerang Heart?" (*Not*, Heart"?)

Dash Inside Quotation Marks

When using a dash to show an interruption or hesitation in speech, put it inside the question mark.

> "Annie! Call security! The gorilla has escap—" yelled the zookeeper.

End comma or no end comma? The Grammar Patrol finds that the dash alone is enough. Some usage experts recommend a comma after the dash: " . . . escap—," yelled . . .

Exclamation Point Inside Quotation Marks

When the exclamation point refers only to the quoted words, it goes inside the quotation mark.

> Rich griped, "Those slobs splattered concrete all over the driveway!"

When ?, –, ! Go Outside

Put these marks (? , —, !) *outside* the quotation marks when they refer to more than the quoted material.

> " . . ."?   " . . ."—   " . . ."!

Question Mark Outside Quotation Marks

When the whole sentence is a question, put the question mark outside the quotation mark.

> Who said, "Nothing ventured, nothing gained"? (*Not*, gained?")

Dash Outside Quotation Marks

Here, the dash separates the quoted words from the snide comment. Put the dash outside the quotation mark.

> "I'll never be caught"—a crook's famous last words. (*Not*, —")

Exclamation Points Outside Quotation Marks

The exclamation point applies to the whole statement. Put it outside the quotation mark.

> He'll never measure up to "Mr. Music"! (*Not*, "Mr. Music!")

Sir Lawrence has a **noble** demeanor. (*Not*, **nobel**—see page 118.)

Quotation Marks with Individual Words

Highlight individual words with separate quotation marks.

Right
Alice Roosevelt had pets named "Josiah," "Algonquin," and "Emily Spinach."

Wrong
Alice Roosevelt had pets named "Josiah, Algonquin, and Emily Spinach."

? **Why?** Set the pets' names off individually to show that they are specific pets with individual names.

Quotation Marks with No and Yes

Don't use quotation marks when using the words "no" and "yes" in a sentence unless they are part of a direct quotation.

Guilford said **yes** (*not* **"yes"**) to wearing Groucho glasses to chair the meeting.

Rosa Parks's simple **no** (*not* **"no"**) has resounded over the decades.

"**Yes**," cried Olivia, "I accept!"

Single Quotation Marks

Single quotation marks (' ') help your reader spot quoted material inside of double quotation marks (" "). Follow the same inside-outside rules on page 165 with single quotation marks.

Single Quotation Marks with Periods and Commas

Periods and commas *always* go inside quotation marks, whether single or double.

Mark Twain said, "Only presidents, editors, and people with tapeworm have the right to use the editorial 'we.' "

MARMADUKE by Brad Anderson

© 2000 United Feature Syndicate, Inc.

9-26

"Don't give me that 'That's *my* chair' look!"

With **regard** to your account . . . (*Not*, **regards**—see page 171)

TIP: Single quotation marks and apostrophes look the same. Below, an apostrophe, not a single quotation mark, takes the place of the final **g** in "leaving." The inside-ouside rules don't apply. Put the period after the apostrophe, as you would after any word that ends a sentence:

> Jimmy John muttered, "I'm leavin'."

Single Quotation Marks with Question Marks
If the question mark applies to the whole question, not just the part in single quotation marks, put the question mark outside the single quotation mark.

> "Didn't they call Andrew Jackson 'Old Hickory'?" Ted asked.

Single Quotation Marks with Exclamation Points
If the exclamation point applies only to words inside the single quotes, the exclamation point goes inside.

> Malik exclaimed, "Toby said, 'Get out!' " (*Not,* out'!" *or* out ' "!)

If the exclamation point applies to the whole sentence, not just the part in single quotation marks, put the exclamation point outside the single quotation mark.

> "Don't call me 'Cupcake'!" yelled Grod the Terminator.

Spacing with Single and Double Quotation Marks
For clarity, put a space between single and double quotation marks: " ' . . .' "

DID YOU KNOW? In the days of typewriters, quotation marks were straight up and down (" "). Only typesetters had access to the fancier curved marks (" "). With today's word processors, you can set your preferences for "smart quotes," also called "curly quotes." These curve like 6s at the beginning of a quotation (" or '). They curve like 9s at the end of a quotation (" or ').

Do use straight quotes (' or "), not curly quotes (' or "), to indicate feet and inches: 5' 7". (The period goes outside here because the quotation mark indicates inches, not a direct quotation.)

The business is run by my partner and **me**. (*Not,* I—see page 149.)

R

REDUNDANCY

THE FUSCO BROTHERS by J.C. Duffy

You can observe a lot by just watching.

—Yogi Berra

Redundancy is the unnecessary duplication of similar words or phrases.

Right
Mel's cauliflower side dish was smelly **as well as** unromantic.

> *or*

Mel's cauliflower side dish was **both** smelly **and** unromantic.

Wrong
The cauliflower side dish was **both** smelly **as well as** unromantic.

? Why? Don't use "both" and "as well as" in same sentence. It's redundant.

Avoid these other common redundancies.

added bonus	octagonal in shape
close proximity	the other alternative
déja vu all over again	refer back to
final result	stubborn in nature
free gift	true fact
in my own personal opinion	truly and sincerely

Neither Tim nor Gerry **is** here. (*Not*, **are**—see page 63.)

Banish redundancies like these:

> as per our discussion (as we said)
>
> Save 50% Off! (Save 50%! *or* 50% Off!)
>
> 3:00 A.M. in the morning (three o'clock in the morning *or* 3 A.M.)
>
> sum total (Choose one or the other.)
>
> each and every (Choose one or the other.)
>
> same identical *or* exact same ("Identical" and "exact" say it all.)
>
> consensus of opinion ("Consensus" means "an agreement of opinion.")
>
> The name of the show is called . . . ("The name of the show is . . ."
> *or* "The show is called . . .")
>
> The reason is because . . . (Use "The reason is . . ." *or* "Because . . .")
>
> What this is is . . . (This is . . .)

DID YOU KNOW? A related term is "pleonasm," which means using too many words to express an idea, such as "at this point in time" for "now." Sometimes a pleonasm is used for emphasis: We heard it with our own ears.

Redundancy and Abbreviations
Technically, "ATM machine," "IPO offering," "PIN number," and "ISBN number" are redundant: "Automated Teller **Machine machine**," "Initial Public **Offering offering**," "Personal Identification **Number number**," "International Standard Book **Number number**."

Likewise, "Please RSVP" means "**Please** respond **please**." ("RSVP" stands for the French *répondez s'il vous plaît,* meaning "Please respond.")

REEK, WREAK
"To reek" means "to smell terrible." "To wreak" means "to inflict or vent." Both are pronounced "reek."

> Their dog Shiloh **reeked** after his encounter with a skunk.

> Mr. Duffleberg **wreaked** his anger on his clerk, Ms. Mynchon.

TIP: Don't confuse "wreak" and "wreck" (as in, "My car's a **wreck**").

> A thunderstorm may **wreak** (*not* **wreck**) havoc on the Buick Invitational.

John's **supposed to** go sailing. (*Not,* **suppose to**—see page 132.)

REGARD, REGARDS

"Regard" and "regards" have specific meanings. As a verb, "regard" means "to look at," "consider in a particular way," or "to hold in affection, esteem." As a noun, "regard" can mean "a look or gaze" or "esteem, affection." "Regards" are good wishes.

> She **regarded** the burned roast with disgust.

> My mother **regards** crossing guards and nurses' aides as saints.

> Grandmother held Eleanor Roosevelt in high **regard**.

> Give my **regards** to Broadway.

"Regard" Phrases

The phrase "with regard to" means "concerning" or "regarding." "With regard to," "as regards," and "in regard to" are common and correct in business writing. You can, however, simplify them: Just substitute "about" or "concerning."

THE BIG E: No one said that English was easy. Do not use "with **regards** to" or "in **regards** to."

REGIMEN, REGIMENT

A "regimen" is a "method or system of cure." A "regiment" is a "unit of soldiers."

> For exercise, many adults are trying an outdoor skipping **regimen**.

> Jackson rejoined his **regiment** at Camp Pendleton.

REGIONALISMS

Soda or pop?	Hot dish or casserole?
Sneakers or tennis shoes?	Supper or dinner?

Where people live affects the meaning and pronunciation of specific words and expressions. These variations, called **regionalisms**, are used most often in informal speech.

One North Carolina man told the Grammar Patrol that when his wife wants to go shopping he "carries [takes] her to the mall."

"How romantic!" said Judith.

Minnesota and North Dakota residents are known to slip "So then," "You betcha," or "Oh, yah!" into sentences, with inflections that carry

The **alternative** is to row across. (*Not*, **other alternative**—see page 169.)

171

subtle differences in meaning. (For more on this, rent the movie *Fargo*.)

Residents of Massachusetts may pronounce Harvard as "Hahvuhd," Cuba as "Cuber," and "park" as "pahk."

Depending on geography, people either "hang up" at the end of a phone conversation or "shut off."

RIGOROUS, VIGOROUS

"Rigorous" means "harsh" or "severe." "Vigorous" means "strong, energetic, robust." Both are adjectives.

> The Guy Fawkes Trail is a **rigorous** hike.

> For **vigorous** exercise, Kim and Mike play squash.

ROOTS (*See prefixes, roots, and suffixes, page 141.*)

RUN-ON SENTENCES (*See incomplete sentences, page 99.*)

S

SALIENT, SALINE

"Salient" means "jutting outward, noticeable, standing out from the rest, prominent": a salient point, a salient angle. "Saline" means "salty."

> Our speaker made three **salient** points in 66 seconds!

> Nurse Ratchet started Melvin on **saline** solution.

SEMANTICS

Eclectic or cluttered?	Plain or homespun?
Humid or sultry?	Dwindled or whittled down?

I **had shown** him my etchings last week. (*Not*, **had showed**—see page 205.)

Semantics is the study of word meanings. Learning the nuances of word meanings can prove challenging. One person may consider a house to be "cramped"; another person might see the same house as "cozy."

Reading can help you fine-tune your vocabulary. A good dictionary will give you a sense of the subtle shades of meaning, feeling, or tone (nuance) among similar words or phrases.

The following semantic pairs are related—their meanings are similar, but not identical: "angry, livid"; "happy, ecstatic"; "loud, deafening"; "like, love."

BIZARRO by Dan Piraro

NON SEQUITUR by Wiley

SEMICOLONS

Semicolons (;) signal a stop. Put one space after a semicolon.
Use semicolons:

▶ To link two closely related thoughts, usually two main (independent) clauses.

> Rolling Readers raised reading scores dramatically; stronger school attendance was an unexpected bonus.

> Jennifer has transformed her front yard; flowers bloom everywhere.

You could also turn these two thoughts into separate sentences.

Helmut has a screw **loose.** (*Not,* **lose**—see page 111.)

▶ To separate a list of items that already includes commas, such as names and titles, cities and states, or cities and countries.

> Congratulations to our new officers: Carolyn Kosonen, president; Jodie Shull, vice president; Suzan Wilson, treasurer; and Julia Ortinez Hansen, secretary.

> The whirlwind, three-day tour includes London, England; Mont Saint Michel and Paris, France; and Frankfurt, Germany.

SENTENCES *(See incomplete sentences, page 99; predicate, page 140; and subject, page 183.)*

A **sentence** expresses a complete thought. A sentence has two parts: a subject and a predicate.

Sentences do one of four jobs.

1. **Declarative** sentences make statements and end with a period.

> Kristi and Som had a baby girl, Malia.

2. **Imperative** sentences give orders and end with a period or an exclamation point.

> **Tell** that obnoxious bully to leave!

> *Hello. My name is Inigo Montoya. You killed my father.* **Prepare** *to die.*
> —*The Princess Bride*

"Tell" and "prepare" give orders. In both examples, the subject "you" is implied: *You* tell. *You* prepare. *(See verbs, page 197.)*

3. **Interrogative** sentences ask questions and end with a question mark.

> Who was Isabella Rossellini's mother? (Answer: Ingrid Bergman.)

4. **Exclamatory** sentences show feelings and end with an exclamation point.

> Hey, Dad! Tony got a job modeling underwear!

Sentences can be **simple, compound,** or **complex.**

▶ A **simple sentence** contains a subject and a predicate.

> **Avery smiles.**
> (subject) (predicate)

This club is **too** crowded! (*Not,* **to** or **two**—see page 188.)

174

Helen bakes pink meringue.

(subject)   (predicate)

▶ A **compound sentence** contains two, linked independent clauses (complete thoughts).
Both clauses have equal weight. Each can stand alone and still make sense. Create compound sentences by joining two complete sentences with a semicolon or with a coordinating conjunction (*and, but, for, nor, or, so, yet*).

She batted her eyelashes; he stopped in mid-sentence.

I am a bear of very little brain, **and** *long words bother me.*

—Winnie the Pooh

TIP: Use a comma to separate clauses in a compound sentence if the subject changes.

I'm going to the awards ceremony, so I had my hair spikes waxed.

(independent clause)   (conjunction)   (independent clause)

▶ A **complex sentence** contains an independent clause with one or more dependent clauses. (*See clauses, page 50.*)

As baby seals basked in the sun, their mothers fished in the cove.

(dependent clause)   (independent clause)

You'd take me salsa dancing if you really loved me.

(independent clause)   (dependent clause)

SERIAL COMMAS (*See commas, page 54.*)

SHALL, WILL

I shall scream, Mr. Bumble, I shall scream.

—Widow Corney, *Oliver*

"Shall" and "will" are helping verbs. There used to be a distinction between "shall" and "will": "I" or "we" was followed by "shall."

We shall let you know when your Tiffany jewels arrive.

Today, this rule is relaxing. In place of the sentences above, it's fine to say "will" with "I" or "we."

We will let you know when your Tiffany jewels arrive.

Fleeting fads **affect** fashion. (*Not,* **effect**—see page 23.)

"Shall" is still used if you are offering or inviting, or if you're indicating something that *must* be done.

> **Shall** we dance?

> We **shall** look forward to seeing you at our Masquerade Ball.

> Bylaws: The books **shall** be audited each December.

SIMILES

To remember what a **simile** is, think of the word "similar," meaning "alike." Similes are figures of speech that compare one thing to another, using the prepositions "like" and "as." (*See also as, like, page 37; figures of speech, page 79; and prepositions, page 143.*)

run like a cheetah	a mind like a computer
smelly as old socks	cantankerous as a bull

SLASHES

The **slash** (/) has many aliases, including "virgule," "solidus," and "diagonal." A slash stands for "or," while a hyphen stands for "and." For example, "every city/state" is not the same as "every city-state." The former gives a choice ("every city or state"), the latter a combination ("city-state" meaning a "sovereign state"). So "2005/06" does not mean two successive years. It means either "2005 or 2006."

Use a slash:

▶ To show the end of a line of poetry when written in narrative, not in stanzas (poetry form).

> "Curtains forcing their will / against the wind / children sleep / exchanging dreams with / seraphim. . . ." ("Awaking in New York," Maya Angelou)

A space is added before and after the slash when showing line breaks in poetry. (Some usage guides prefer a space only after the slash.)

▶ With fractions.

1/3	3/8	15/16

Here's a catalog for serious **cooks**. (*Not*, **cooks'**—see page 135.)

▶ For dates, informally.

| 6/1/05 | 8/13/73 | 4/30/67 |

DID YOU KNOW? A slash is also used in the dating of years in Greek antiquity. You would write "455/456 B.C.," because the Greek new year began in mid-year, not January.

▶ To show two options.
Don't put a space before or after the slash.

| pass/fail seminar | win/win situation |
| credit/noncredit course | thumbs up/thumbs down |

▶ In Web site addresses.

http://www.grammarpatrol.com/

TIP: Do not substitute a slash for a dash. (*See dashes, page 66.*)

SMART QUOTES (*See quotation marks, page 163.*)

SOME DAY, SOMEDAY
"Some day" (two words) means "a specific, but unnamed day." "Someday" (one word) means "at some time in the future."

I'll clean out my closet **some day** soon.

Someday, Sheila plans to parachute from a plane.

SOME TIME, SOMETIME, SOMETIMES
"Some time," "sometime," and "sometimes" are adverbs: They answer the question "when?" "Some time" means "an indefinite period." "Sometime" means "an unspecified point in time." "Sometimes" means "now and then."

That fuzz-covered broccoli died **some time** ago.

Tami hopes to visit California **sometime**.

Sometimes I eat pizza for breakfast.

Kitty **sneaked** down for a midnight snack. (*Not*, **snuck**—see page 205.)

SPELLING (*See homonyms, page 87; plurals, page 133; and possessives, page 137.*)

Quick Spelling Quiz

☐ **maladjusted** *or* ☐ **malajusted?**

☐ **temperment** *or* ☐ **temperament?**

☐ **acommodate** *or* ☐ **accommodate?**

☐ **committee** *or* ☐ **commitee?**

☐ **debatable** *or* ☐ **debateable?**

☐ **yeild** *or* ☐ **yield?**

☐ **hurtful** *or* ☐ **hurtfull?**

☐ **reluctent** *or* ☐ **reluctant?**

☐ **irrisistable** *or* ☐ **irresistible?**

☐ **precede** *or* ☐ **preceed?**

☐ **arrangement** *or* ☐ **arrangment?**

☐ **ocassion** *or* ☐ **occasion?**

☐ **cantaloupe** *or* ☐ **canteloupe?**

☐ **occurance** *or* ☐ **occurrence?**

(*See page 181 for answers.*)

Some people are born good spellers. Others struggle with it. The good news is that spelling is not related to intelligence.

A Classics professor notes that back in the mid-20th century, when many more students took Latin, they grew familiar with the Latin roots that appear in about two-thirds of English. This made students more adept at spelling. (*See prefixes, roots, suffixes, page 141.*)

Spell Checkers and Misspeller's Dictionaries

"Look it up," you're told. But how can you look it up if you don't know the spelling? Dictionaries such as *Webster's New World Pocket Misspeller's Dictionary* are written especially for anyone who's spelling impaired. You look up the word the way you think it *might* be spelled. Bingo! Often, you not only find the word spelled *your* way, but you'll find the correct spelling,

The elephant waved **its** trunk. (*Not,* **it's**—see page 105.)

too. On the Internet, use dictionary sites, such as www.m-w.com or others. If the word you enter is spelled wrong, you'll be given several close hits. You can also use wild cards: "cant*l*pe" finds "cantaloupe."

Like it or not, your spelling affects your image. If spelling is your weakness, ask a friend or colleague to proof your work and use your spell checker faithfully—it's a great tool. Spell-check every document you write on the computer, and every letter and email you send, to avoid errors such as writing "ne**cc**esary" for "ne**c**essary," "co**mmitt**ment" for "co**mmit**ment," "emba**rass**" for "emba**rrass**," or "mispell" for "mis**s**pell."

But that same trusty spell checker can't tell "grin and *bear* it" from "grin and *bare* it." It can't know that you meant "kangaroos" where you wrote "kangaroo."

DID YOU KNOW? Popular groups, companies, and sports teams often tweak spelling and punctuation rules to create unusual names.

Boyz II Men	OutKast	Led Zeppelin
Rice Krispies	White Sox	Operalia 2000

FOR BETTER OR FOR WORSE by Lynn Johnston

Power Up Your Spelling Skills

Here are a few things you can do to improve your spelling:

▶ Pronounce words carefully. (*See pronunciation, page 157.*)

▶ Don't add or subtract syllables when you say a word. "Athlete" doesn't have an extra syllable. Say, "ath´ lete," *not* "ath´ uh lete." "Mathematics" does have an **e** in the middle. Say, "math eh ma´ tics," *not* "math ma´ tics."

Jack and Jill **go** up the hill. (*Not,* goes—see page 26.)

▶ Know basic spelling rules.
Here's a sampling:

- ▸ A silent **e** at the end of a word makes the vowel before it long. ("Hat" becomes "hate"; "sit" becomes "site"; "sham" becomes "shame.")

- ▸ To pluralize words ending in **y** with a consonant before it, change the **y** to **i** and add **es**: party, parties.

- ▸ Use **i** before **e** except after **c** unless sounding like **ā** as in "neighbor" or "weigh."

  i before *e*: field, yield, sieve

  e follows *c*: ceiling, receive, deceit

  sounds like *a*: rein, weight, sleigh

  TIP: "When two vowels go walking, the first one does the talking." Remember this ditty from grade school? It almost always works. When vowels are paired, say the name of the first vowel. The second vowel is silent:

  gait (say the long **a** sound)
  dream (say the long **e** sound)
  skies (say the long **i** sound)
  float (say the long **o** sound)

- ▸ To change most words ending in **e** to adjectives, cross off the **e** and add a **y**:

  smoke/smoky
  stone/stony
  spice/spicy
  sponge/spongy

THE BIG E: A few words don't follow this rule: "Dice" becomes "dicey," for instance. And, of all things, Smokey the Bear has an **e**.

REAL LIFE ADVENTURES by Wise and Aldrich

UM, NO, WAIT...

Spelling tip: It's I before E—except when it doesn't look right.

Senator Mudd used bribery to **alter** votes. (*Not*, altar—see page 27.)

- Use mnemonics (nee mon´ iks), or memory aids.
  Here are two good ones:

  ▸ Think "four" (4) with fourth, the number after "third." You won't confuse it with "forth," as in "go *forth.* " (Note that you capitalize "fourth" in "*Fourth* of July" and that the number "forty" has no ***u***.)

  ▸ "Weird" is weird! With this "*i* before *e*" rule-breaker, the *e* comes before the *i*. Think, "We are weird," and you'll remember that "weird" starts with "we."

- Know the difference between nouns (cloth, clothes; breath) and verbs (clothe; breathe).

- Focus on your own spelling demons! Write down the words you often spell incorrectly; refer to them often. For example, maybe you'll note that "advertise," "exercise," and "surprise" end in ***se***, while "prize" ends in ***ze***.

RUBES by Leigh Rubin

"Yesiree! Finished it in five minutes flat!"

PS How did you do on the Quick Spelling Quiz? **The answers**: *maladjusted, temperament, accommodate, committee, debatable, yield, hurtful, reluctant, irresistible, precede, arrangement, occasion, cantaloupe, occurrence.*

SPLIT INFINITIVES (*See verbs, page 192.*)

SPOKEN ERRORS (*See fillers, page 80, and pronunciation, page 157.*)
The way you speak is a reflection of you. If a lawyer says, "Between you and I" or "Me and you know better" in a closing argument in a courtroom, listeners may focus more on the incorrect grammar than on the ideas behind the words. In casual speech, you or your colleagues can get away with bloopers. In formal writing and speech—school, business, or public speaking—such errors detract from your professional image.

An **antidote** for snake bites is antivenin. (*Not,* **anecdote**—see page 29.)

Follow these rules to avoid mistakes heard frequently in speech:

▶ Don't say, "alls" for "all," "get ahold of" for "get," or "looking to" for "planning to" or "hoping for."

> "**All** I have to do is feed the iguana." (*Not,* "**Alls** I gotta do . . .")

> "I can't **get** (or **find**) the red paint." (*Not,* "I can't **get ahold of**" *or* "I can't get **aholt of** . . .")

> "I'm **hoping for** a promotion." (*Not,* "I'm **looking to be** promoted.")

▶ Don't use "go" when you mean "say":

> "So then, he **says**, 'Take it or leave it.' " (*Not,* "So then, he **goes** . . .")

Likewise, please, please, don't use "went" for "said."

> "So then I **said**, 'Evander Holyfield's better than Lennox Lewis!' " (*Not,* "So then I **went** . . .")

▶ Don't add extra words.

> "That's too long a skit." (*Not,* "That's too long **of** a skit.")

> "That's too wide an SUV." (*Not,* "That's too wide **of** an SUV.")

▶ Don't leave out a word.

> "I have a couple **of** ideas." (*Not,* "I have a couple ideas.")

▶ Don't use "there's" (meaning "there is") with plurals. (*See subject-verb agreement, page 26.*)

> "**There are** lots of quacks." (*Not,* "**There's** lots of quacks.")

▶ Don't let verbs and subjects disagree in number.

> "Elvis **suspenders are** crucial to my outfit." (*Not,* "Elvis **suspenders is** crucial . . .")

▶ Don't say, "Where ya at?" Say, "Where are you?" instead.

▶ Don't leave a phrase unfinished.

> "**As far as** slippers **are concerned** (*or* **go**), I prefer piggies to moose." (*Not,* "**As far as** slippers . . .")

The Simmonses love Maui **anyway**. (*Not,* **anyways**—see page 30.)

TIP: The phrase "as for" doesn't need more words to be complete: "**As for** slippers, I prefer piggies to moose."

▶ Don't use "like" when you mean "as." (*See as, like, page 37.*)

"**As** I said, Red's about as graceful as a barge." (*Not*, "**Like** I said . . .")

▶ Don't forget the subjunctive. (*See subjunctive mood, page 197.*)

"If I **were** you, I'd bunt." (*Not*, "If I **was** you . . .")

▶ Don't double your negatives. (*See double negatives, page 116.*)

"I **can hardly** wait." (*Not*, "I **can't hardly** wait.)

▶ Don't forget "from" with "graduate" if an object follows.

Lena **graduated from** Yale. (*Not*, **graduated** Yale.)

TIP: You can use "graduate" if no object follows: Lena **graduated** in May.

SUBJECT (*See predicate, page 140, and sentences, page 174.*)
A **subject** tells who or what a sentence or clause is about.

Simple Subject

The **toilet** overflowed.
(*subject*)

Complete Subject
A complete subject includes the subject and all the words that describe it.

The nervous, would-be dancer did a pirouette during his audition.
(*complete subject*)

Compound Subject

There was a time when **a fool and his money** *were soon parted, but now it happens to everybody.*

—Adlai Stevenson

Like "a fool and his money," a compound subject has two or more words or phrases joined by the conjunction "and." Use a plural verb with a compound subject.

Daffy, Mickey, and Minnie ride the Matterhorn after hours.
(*They* ride.)

Sign: Game **tickets** sold here (*Not*, **ticket's**—see page 135.)

SUBJECT COMPLEMENTS *(See linking verbs, page 196; predicate adjectives, page 140; and predicate nouns, page 141.)*

Subject complements are nouns, adjectives, or pronouns that follow linking verbs.

Nouns as Subject Complements

> Marie Curie **became** a **scientist**.
>   *(linking verb)*   *(subject complement—noun)*

Adjectives as Subject Complements

> Restaurateur Nobuyuki Matsuhisa **is versatile**.
>   *(linking verb) (subject complement—adjective)*

Pronouns as Subject Complements

When pronouns follow forms of the linking verbs "to be," use the subjective form of a pronoun. (In Grammarspeak, "to be" verbs are called "verbs of being": *am, is, are, was, were.*)

Here's a review of subjective pronouns.

Subjective Pronouns

Person	*Singular*	*Plural*
First	I	we
Second	you	you
Third	he, she, it	they

> It **is they** who snarfed down all the cashews.
> *(linking verb) (subject complement—subjective pronoun)*

> The belle of the Snowflake Ball **was she**.
>   *(linking verb) (subject complement—subjective pronoun)*

"It is I" or "It is me"?

Informally, especially in spoken language, saying "It is *me*" or "It's *me*" has become acceptable, even though "It is *I*" is more correct. The Grammar Patrol sticks with the latter.

Bertha **lets** Alden win at chess. (*Not,* **let's**—see page 109.)

MNEMONIC (MEMORY AID): To remember the meaning of "complement," think of the word "complete." The words in a subject **complement complete** the subject of the sentence.

SUBJUNCTIVE *(See verbs, page 197.)*

SUBSTANDARD WORDS

Some words seem like real words, but aren't. They've been created by stretching, mispronouncing, or changing a real word. Avoid using substandard words.

Standard Words	Substandard Words
all right	alright
analysis	analyzation
anyway	anyways
consternation	connerstation
integral	intregal
oriented	orientated
regardless	irregardless
relevant, relevance	revelant, revelance
remuneration	renumeration
supposedly	supposably
unequivocally	unequivocably

SUCH AS *(See like, such as, page 110.)*

SUFFIXES *(See prefixes, roots, and suffixes, page 141.)*

SYNTAX *(See diagramming sentences, page 70.)*

FRANK AND ERNEST by Bob Thaves

WORDS DOWN GOT WE'VE GOOD PRETTY -- SHOULD NOW INVENT WE SYNTAX!

© 1997 by NEA, Inc. THAVES
E-Mail: FandE BobT @AOL.COM 10-11

Interactive Frank and Ernest ®
www.unitedmedia.com

The expert **appraised** the wax doll. (*Not,* **apprised**—see page 34.)

Syntax is the structure of language: the way words fit together to create meaning. Errors in syntax result in confusing sentences.

Incorrect Syntax:
Chocolate and other sweets **break out my face**. (The sweets don't break out; your face does. Two key words—"make my"—are missing.)

The Fix:
Chocolate and other sweets **make my face break out**.

Incorrect Syntax:
Have a good trip **wherever your final destination may take you**. (A destination can't take you anywhere.)

The Fix:
Have a good trip **wherever you may travel from here**.

Incorrect Syntax:
I hate when that happens. (The pronoun "it" is missing.)

The Fix:
I hate **it** when that happens."

Tangled syntax makes readers or listeners work harder. When you know the job each word does in a sentence, you have an intuitive sense of how words fit together. The more you read and play with words, the easier language becomes.

Here are some syntax basics:

▶ Every complete sentence has a subject and a predicate. (*See predicate, page 140; sentences, page 174; and subject, page 183.*)

    The **storm raged**.
      (*subject*) (*predicate*)

▶ Words need to be combined in logical ways.
"Raged storm the" uses the same three words as above, but the mixed-up syntax destroys the meaning.

▶ When the syntax and or punctuation changes, the meaning changes.
The same words in different order can mean completely different things.

    "Do I love you?" (Doubt is creeping in.)

    "I do love you!" (There's no doubt about it.)

I **knew** you'd paint your room purple. (*Not,* **knowed**—see page 204.)

People learning English may have trouble with English syntax, especially if the structure is not the same as it is in their native languages.

English language learners might say, "I'm *glad* with my game," when they mean, "I'm *happy* with my game," *or* "I'm glad I played well." Word order may differ, too.

In Spanish: *Te amo.* (Word-for-word translation: "You I love.")

In French: *Je t'aime.* (Word-for-word translation: "I you love.")

In English: I love you.

T

TENANT, TENET

A "tenant" is "a renter or occupant." A "tenet" is "an opinion or principle."

My **tenant** cooks with too much garlic.

"Eat dessert first" is one of Wendy's lifelong **tenets**.

TENSE (*See verbs, page 201.*)

THEIR, THERE, THEY'RE

"Their" is a possessive pronoun.

Their snail crossed the finish line first.

"There" shows place; you can also use "there" to start a sentence.

On your coin map, the Peach Tree State quarter goes **there**.

There are two people in that giraffe costume.

"They're" is the contraction of "they are."

They're going to Las Vegas to be married. (*They are* going.)

I **couldn't** care less about T-Ball. (*Not*, **could**—see page 116.)

TIP: Don't confuse "theirs" and "there's," either.

> The choice between pork bellies and futures is **theirs**. (possessive)

> **There's** plenty of pecan pie left. (*There is* plenty.)

TIME AND MONEY

▶ Leave out the minutes when writing about the time on the hour (i.e., when the minute hand points at twelve or the digital clock's minute display reads "00").

> 3 A.M. (*not* 3:00 A.M.)

▶ Use the possessive with time and money words. (*See possessives, page 137.*)

> an hour**'s** delay = a delay **of** an **hour** (singular possessive)

> a few days**'** quiet = a quiet **of** a few **days** (plural possessive)

> six months**'** probation = a probation **of** six **months** (plural posessive)

> a penny**'s** worth = a worth **of** a **penny** (singular possessive)

> fifty dollars**'** worth = a worth **of** fifty **dollars** (plural possessive)

THE BIG E: Some time phrases don't show possession—no apostrophe needed.

> three weeks later
> six months earlier

TIP: Use words, not numerals, with the word "o'clock": **six** o'clock, *not* **6** o'clock.

TO, TOO, TWO

"To" helps form the infinitive of a verb: Jeremy hoped **to dazzle** Sara with his tap dancing.

"Too" means "also": Marge loves leftovers, **too**.

"Two" refers to the number 2: I have **two** precious parakeets.

TOWARD, TOWARDS

While "towards" is still acceptable, it's more British. We prefer "toward."

The Déja Vu team won last **fall**. (*Not*, **Fall**—see page 48.)

U

UNIQUE *(See adjectives, page 17.)*

V

VAIN, VANE, VEIN

The adjective "vain" means "fruitless or hollow" (a **vain** endeavor) or "conceited" (a **vain** person). For "vane," think "weather vane." It indicates wind direction. The noun "vein" is a blood vessel carrying blood back to the heart.

> "You're so **vain**," sang Carly Simon. "You probably think this song is about you."

> The nurse searched for Dracula's **vein** to draw blood.

VERBALS *(See verbs, page 205.)*

VERBS *(This hefty verb section is organized alphabetically, by topic.)*

Verbs show action ("skitter," "chop," "zoom," "flip") or a state of being (the verb "to be": am, is, are, was, were).

Verbs power sentences. Choose active, specific verbs to make your writing strong: "scramble," "strum," "ski."

The form and spelling of a verb depend on its tense, person, number, mood, and voice.

> **Tense:** past, present, future (and other more complex tenses)
> **Person:** first, second, or third
> **Number:** singular or plural
> **Mood:** indicative, imperative, or subjunctive
> **Voice:** active or passive

The week **passed** fast. (*Not,* **past**—see page 127.)

Active Voice and Passive Voice (*See voice, active and passive, page 208.*)

Auxiliary Verbs (*See helping verbs, page 191.*)

"Being" Verbs (*See verbs of being, page 208.*)

Contractions (*See also apostrophes, page 30, and double negatives, page 116.*)
Contractions are shortcuts—two words "pulled together" or **contract**ed into
one—used in speech, dialogue, and informal writing. One of the combined
words is a verb, and an apostrophe holds the place of omitted letter(s).

does not = doesn't	you will = you'll
she is = she's	it is = it's
had not = hadn't	who is = who's
I've = I have	we will = we'll
will not = won't	

Some contractions have different meanings, depending on the words
around them. "What's" can mean "what is." Add a participle and "what's"
means "what has."

> **What's** (**What is**) the origin of black holes in the universe?

> **What's** (**What has**) Slippery Jim **done** now?

Contraction or Possessive Pronoun?
Don't confuse contractions with possessive pronouns. Contractions have
apostrophes. Possessive pronouns don't!

Contractions are Shortcuts (*Uses an apostrophe*)	Possessives Show Ownership (*No apostrophe*)
It's = It is *or* **it has** "It's another win for the team!"	**Its** The Grissini Grill plugs its cioppino.
You're = You are You're (you are) my only uncle.	**Your** I love your Tag watch.
They're = They are They're (they are) swing dancers.	**Their** Their TV broke, thank goodness.

"Cuddles, lie down!" (*Not*, lay—see page 194.)

Be on the alert for accidental mix-ups like these:

> "**Your** now entering Harmony." (Should be "You're": **You are.**)

> Call Bugbusters. **Their** available 24/7. (Should be "They're": **They are.**)

> Motherhood has **it's** privileges. (Should be "its" privileges: for ownership.)

Noun-Verb Contractions

Informally, a noun or pronoun can be part of a contraction.

> **Mike's** taking Connor for a bike ride. (**Mike is** taking Connor for a bike ride.)

> **She's** a great trapeze artist. (**She is** a great trapeze artist.)

Contraction Quicksand *(See got, have, page 84.)*

When chatting with friends, you might say, "We **should've** (should have) bet on the Knicks." This spoken contraction often leads to writing and saying "should **of**," "could **of**," or "would **of**." Avoid this incorrect combination in speech and writing. (Don't use "should've," "would've," and "could've" unless you're writing dialogue.)

Gerund *(See phrases, page 133; possessive pronouns and gerunds, page 150; and verbals, page 205.)*

When an *ing* form of a verb has the job of a noun, it's called a **gerund**.

> Sierra, a novice skier, focused on **snowplowing**.

Helping Verbs

Helping verbs (in Grammarspeak, "auxiliary verbs") work together with other verbs. They include forms of "be," "have," "can," and "will": *am, is, are, was, were, be, been, has, have, had, can, could, will, would, shall, should, may, might, must,* and *ought.*

> I **am exhausted** from my week in Bimini.
> (*helping verb*) (*verb*)

> "I **must have** slept," decided Rip Van Winkle.
> (*helping verb*) (*verb*)

> We **will watch** Cokie Roberts's interview tonight.
> (*helping verb*) (*verb*)

Ike's flip-flops **complement** his beach attire. (*Not*, **compliment**—see page 60.)

Infinitives *(See verbals, page 205.)*

An **infinitive** is the "to" form of a verb: "to bellow," "to dig," "to skid." (It's called an infinitive because it is "not limited" to person or number: It's "infinite." You don't say, "we to bellow.")

Infinitives can act as subjects, objects, or complements (modifiers).

> **To Rollerblade** is my life. (The infinitive acts as the subject of the sentence.
>
> The Dixie Chicks were the group **to see.** (The infinitive modifies the noun "group.")

To Split or Not to Split

The old rule about never splitting infinitives—putting other words between the "to" and the base form—no longer holds. This rule originally stemmed from Latin grammar. Latin infinitives are one word (*amare* is "to love"), so they cannot be split. In English, **to** occasionally **split** (like that!) an infinitive is okay. If you can write the sentence differently, do so. Otherwise, leave the split, as in this famous Star Trek line: "**To** boldly **go** where no one has gone before."

DID YOU KNOW? With infinitive phrases, avoid substituting "and" for "to." Say "Call **to** schedule a termite inspection," *not* "Call **and** schedule a termite inspection."

Intransitive and Transitive Verbs

Verbs are either intransitive or transitive.

▶ **Intransitive verbs** do not take a direct object.

> The crowd **rose.**

The verb "rose" is intransitive. You can't say, "The crowd **rose** itself", or "The crowd **rose** excitement." The verb "rose" takes no object.

Intransitive verbs can be followed by adverbs that tell *how, when, why,* or *to what extent.*

> **appears slowly** **belong completely** **looked wistfully**

The change in Conan's attitude was **negligible.** (*Not,* **negligent**—see page 118.)

MNEMONIC (MEMORY AID): For "transitive," think of the word "transit." It means "to go across." A transitive verb's activity "crosses over" to an object. "In" means "not," so **in**transitive" means "does *not* cross over." **Intransitives** do *not* take an **object**.

▶ **Transitive verbs** take a direct object.

> Kobe Bryant **scored** a three-pointer.

The verb "scored" is transitive. The direct object, "three-pointer," receives the action of the verb "scored." Kobe scored what? A three-pointer.

DID YOU KNOW? When looking up verbs in the dictionary, you may come across the abbreviations *vt.* and *vi.* The abbreviation "*vi.*" indicates "intransitive verb" and the abbreviation "*vt.*" indicates "transitive verb."

> Dictionary entry: "skid, *vt.*"

> Dictionary entry: "appear, *vi.*"

Easily Confused Pairs

Three easily confused pairs of intransitive and transitive verbs are "lie" and "lay, " "rise" and "raise," and "sit" and "set."

lie (no object)	lay your sunglasses here (object)
rise (no object)	raise the roof (object)
sit (no object)	set my hair (object)

SYLVIA by Nicole Hollander

Country music is **different from** opera. (*Not,* **different than**—see page 72.)

Lay, Lie

Present Tense	Present Participle	Past Tense *(no helping verb)*	Past Participle *(needs a helping verb)*
lie *(to recline, be situated—takes no object)*	lying	lay	lain
lay *(to put down, place, arrange some-thing— takes an object)*		laying	laid laid

Say, "Lie down, Bruno," *not* "Lay down, Bruno." (Dogs have a sixth sense about good grammar.)

People often confuse "lie" and "lay." Check out these examples:

Lie

Present	He lies (*not* lays) on the couch.
	He is lying (*not* is laying) on the couch.
Past	He lay (*not* laid) down yesterday.
	He had lain (*not* had laid) down yesterday.
Future	She will lie (*not* will lay) on the beach.
	She will be lying (*not* will be laying) on the beach.

(The verb "lie" also means to tell a falsehood; as a noun, it means "a fib.")

TIP: Seams **lie** flat, not **lay** flat. (No object follows "lie.")

Lay

Present	Lay (*not* lie) your CDs on the table, James.
	James is laying (*not* is lying) the CDs on the table.
Past	James laid (*not* lay) the CDs on the table yesterday.
	James had laid (*not* had lain) the CDs on the table yesterday.
Future	They will lay (*not* will lie) the tile floor soon.
	They will have laid (*not* will have lain) the tile floor soon.

TIP: Substitute the word "place" for "lay." If "place" works, it's correct. Otherwise, use "lie."

The cheese had **fermented** to green fuzz. (*Not*, **fomented**—see page 78.)

Raise, Rise

Present Tense	Present Participle	Past Tense *(no helping verb)*	Past Participle *(needs a helping verb)*
rise *(to get up—takes no object)*	rising	rose	risen
raise *(to move higher— takes an object)*	raising	raised	raised

The sun **is rising**. (no object)

Artie **raised** his pirate **flag** on a broomstick pole. (object)

TIP: Dough **rises**, *not* **raises**. (No object follows "rises.")

Sit, Set

Present Tense	Present Participle	Past Tense *(no helping verb)*	Past Participle *(needs a helping verb)*
sit *(to be seated— takes no object)*	sitting	sat	sat
set *(to put down, place, arrange—takes an object)*	setting	set set	

"**Sit** here, Uncle Jethro." (no object)

"Don't **set** your **dentures** on the back step, Uncle Jethro." (object)

THE BIG E: "Set" has many meanings. It can also mean "to harden" (concrete **sets**) and "drop below the horizon" (the sun **sets**).

Irregular Verbs *(See verb forms, regular and irregular, page 202.)*

The new drug **homed** in on leukemia. (*Not,* **honed**—see page 87.)

Linking Verbs *(See predicate adjectives, page 140, and subject complements, page 184.)*
Linking verbs include "to be" verbs, verbs of the senses, and some other verbs.

▶ "To be" linking verbs include *am, is, are, was,* and *were.*

> **Bitsy was** a cantankerous **sow.**
> *(subject) (linking verb)   (predicate noun)*

> **It is I.**
> *(subject)(linking verb)(pronoun)*

▶ Verbs of the senses—*look, feel, sound, taste,* and *smell*—are linking verbs. Words that follow verbs of the senses also complete the meaning of the subject.

> **Sight:** That sushi **looks** fabulous. (fabulous sushi)
> **Touch:** A facial scrub **feels** scratchy. (scratchy scrub)
> **Hearing:** That electric guitar **sounds** off-key. (off-key guitar)
> **Taste:** Your hot fudge sundaes **taste** divine. (divine sundae)
> **Smell:** The cabin **smelled** stuffy. (stuffy cabin)

▶ Other verbs, such as *become, seem, appear, believe, grow, remain,* and *prove* are also linking verbs.

> **Nelson Mandela became** South Africa's **hero.**
>
> *(subject)   (linking verb)   (predicate noun)*

> The **jazz trio proved popular** at Nico's party.
>
> *(subject)(linking verb)(predicate adjective)*

Mood

What kind of a **mood** is your verb in? No, this doesn't mean grumpy, romantic, or down in the dumps. Verbs have three moods: **indicative, imperative,** and **subjunctive.** You can tell a verb's mood by its form.

The **indicative** mood is used for facts. If your verb tells a fact or asks something factual, it's in the indicative mood. The **imperative** mood (from the Latin for "command") is used for commands. If a verb sounds downright bossy, it's in the imperative mood. The **subjunctive** mood is used for non-facts. If a verb expresses a wish or something nonfactual or contrary to fact, it's in the subjunctive mood.

Did Joe **marinate** this beef in motor oil? (*Not,* **marinade**—see page 112.)

Indicative Mood (Declarative or Interrogative)

In the **indicative mood**, verbs either make statements (they declare or tell) or ask questions (they interrogate or ask).

▶ Declarative sentences give a fact or opinion.

> Toto **will carry** Dorothy's slippers.

▶ Interrogative sentences ask questions.

> **Do** you **like** green eggs and ham?

> **Did** Jack **meet** Jill tumbling down the hill?

Note the format of the interrogatives: The verbs "like" and "meet" both have a helper, "do" and "did," that appears before the subject. Be on the lookout for an asking adverb, another clue to the interrogative mood: *who, when, where, how, who,* and *why.*

> **Who** was that masked man?

Imperative Mood

In the **imperative mood**, verbs give orders or make requests.

> *Hold fast to dreams . . .*
>
> —Langston Hughes, "Dreams"

The subject for these imperative mood verbs is often implied. An imperative sentence can be just one word long. Such one-word sentences may end with exclamation points.

[You] Run!	[You] Be careful.
[You] Leave, Roger!	[You] Unplug the sink!

Subjunctive Mood

In the **subjunctive mood**, verbs express a wish, request, recommendation, or something contrary to fact.

You'll remember the subjunctive mood if you think of Tevye in the musical *Fiddler on the Roof* singing, "If I **were** a rich man . . ." Tevye is not rich: The sentence is contrary to fact, so it calls for the subjunctive "were." (*Not,* "If I **was.**")

Substituting "were" for "was" in "if" clauses is the most common use of the subjunctive.

Lord Cuspid is homelier **than** a possum. (*Not,* then—see page 64.)

Right
If I **were** you, I'd give up day trading.

Wrong
If I **was** you, I'd give up day trading.

? **Why?** The person speaking ("I") is not the day trader. The statement is contrary to fact. Use the subjunctive "were."

TIP: Not all "if" clauses take the subjunctive. You can use "was" with "if" to show the past tense.

> If George Clooney **was** in that limo, I didn't see him.

Also use the subjunctive:

▶ With verbs followed by "that," such as *demand, insist, recommend, request, suggest,* and *urge.* (Use "be," plus a participle.)

> We **recommend that** more fog **be used** in Scene II.

▶ With a "to be" verb in the present tense.
If using a subjunctive "to be" verb in the present tense, the form is "be." To form a present tense "to be" subjunctive, use the word "be" plus a past participle.

> Alas, it **is** necessary that our Siberian cruise **be postponed.**

▶ With other verbs in the present tense.
With other verbs, present or past, use the present form of the subjunctive: It has no **s**, even in the third person singular.

> Our dress code **requires** that every employee **wear** (*not* **wears**) a suit.
>   (*present*)   (*present subjunctive*)

> Santa **suggested** that Techno-Elf **create** (*not* **creates**) a new jet ski.
>   (*past*)   (*present subjunctive*)

▶ With wishes.
In the subjunctive mood, use the past tense to express a wish.

> The Baldwins **wish** they **had memorized** their scripts.
>   (*present*)   (*past subjunctive*)

> Tim **wished** he **were** old enough to drive a hook and ladder.
>   (*past*) (*past subjunctive*)

▶ With "had" or "would have" in "if" clauses about imagined conditions.

You don't need to buy **anything**! (*Not,* **nothing**—see page 116.)

Right

If Marcy **had** persisted, she **would have** ridden the surfboard.

or

Had Marcy persisted, she **would have** ridden the surfboard.

Wrong

If Marcy **would have** persisted, she **would have** ridden the surfboard.

? Why? Don't double up on the form "would have" for the subjunctive. Instead, use the form "had" plus "would have" in "if" clauses about things that could have happened, but didn't. Marcy had given up on surfing, so the statement is imagined.

Number and Person

Verbs have number (one or more than one) and person (first, second, or third). The present tense chart below shows how this works.

	Number	
Person	*Singular (One)*	*Plural (More than one)*
First	I see	we see
Second	you see	you see
Third	he sees, she sees, it sees	they see

TIP: In the present tense, third person singular verbs end in *s* or *es*.
He passes!   She shoots!   She scores!

Third Person Singular (He, She, It)

Right

He runs fast.
She runs fast.
It runs fast.

Wrong

He run fast.
She run fast.
It run fast.

DID YOU KNOW? The demonstrative pronouns "this" and "that" are singular; "these" and "those" are plural.

This wrinkles easily. (Use a third person singular verb form.)

These wrinkle easily. (Use a third person plural verb form.)

Here are Bridget and I at the Blarney Stone. (*Not*, me—see page 184.)

199

Participles (*See dangling participial phrases, page 65; verb forms, regular and irregular, page 202; and verbals, page 205.*)
All verbs have a participial form. **Participles** can be part of a verb (is **tripping**, had **tripped**) or act as modifiers (**dripping** faucet, **canoeing** skills).

Present Participles

To form the **present participle**, add *ing* to a present tense verb. Presto! A present participle.

> punting   walking   thinking

If the verb has a consonant-plus-*e* ending, drop the *e* and add *ing*.

> hope, hoping   spike, spiking   believe, believing

If a verb has a vowel-consonant ending, double the last letter, then add *ing*.

> spin, spinning   run, running   flap, flapping

THE BIG E: This rule isn't 100 percent foolproof. With "show," for instance, just add *ing*: "showing."

Past Participles

To form the **past participle** with regular verbs, add *d* or *ed* to the verb form: skat**ed**, croon**ed**, plaster**ed**. Irregular verbs don't follow that rule. *(See the list of irregular verbs, page 203.)*

Perfect Participles

To form the **perfect participle**, connect a participle with "having" or "having been." Perfect participles signal that something happened before the action of the main verb.

> **Having played** doubles at the Olympics, Venus and Serena Williams continued their separate tennis careers. ("Having" makes this the **active voice**.)

> **Having been thrown** out of the restaurant, Tony settled for Spaghettios. ("Having been" makes this the **passive voice**.)

Chase and Connor **play** in the sandbox. (*Not,* **plays**—see page 26.)

Participial Phrases as Modifiers *(See dangling participial phrases, page 65.)*
Add other words to a participle to create a **participial phrase**.

> **Running the red light**, the **car** was caught on a minicam.
> (Present participial phrase acting as an adjective, modifying "car.")

> **Lighted only by the moon**, the **path** was treacherous.
> (Past participial phrase acting as an adjective, modifying "path.")

Passive Voice *(See voice, active and passive, page 208.)*

Past Participles *(See participles, page 200.)*

Person *(See number and person, page 199.)*

Phrasal Verbs *(See phrasals, page 130.)*

Regular Verbs *(See verb forms, regular and irregular, page 202.)*

Split Infinitives *(See infinitives, page 192.)*

Subject-Verb Agreement *(See subject-verb agreement, page 26.)*

Subjunctive *(See mood, page 196.)*

Substandard Verb Forms *(See verb forms, regular and irregular, page 202.)*

Tense

ONE BIG HAPPY by Rick Detorie

Verbs are versatile. They change forms to indicate *when* something happens.

Present Tense	Past Tense	Future Tense
Dogs bark.	Dogs barked.	Dogs will bark.

Julie's snapdragons **grew** tall. (*Not,* **growed**—see page 204.)

Add a helping verb to create a verb that shows something that happens before or after another event:

Present Perfect Tense	Past Perfect Tense	Future Perfect Tense
Dogs have barked.	Dogs had barked.	Dogs will have barked.

Verb Forms, Regular and Irregular

Every verb has a form for the present tense, present participle, past tense, and past participle. It's important to know whether a verb is **regular** (they're the easy ones!) or **irregular**.

Regular verbs

Regular verbs follow a pattern. Add *d* or *ed* to the present tense of a verb to form the past tense and the past participle. The past participle takes a helping verb.

Present Tense	Past Tense	Past Perfect Tense
paint	painted	**had** paint**ed**
snap	snapped	**had** snapp**ed**
speculate	speculated	**had** speculated

Irregular verbs

But some verbs don't follow the regular pattern above. They are **irregular**. (*See the list of irregular verbs, page 203.*)

Substandard Verb Forms

You would think that if one irregular verb says "drink, drank, drunk," you could also say, "think, thank, thunk." But English is far too slippery for that. It's "think, thought, **thought**."

You can't invent a past participle, either. "Brang," "broughten," "brung," "drug," "slidden," "slunken," "swang," or "wroten" aren't acceptable in standard English, although they may be heard in some regional speech.

Young children or people learning English often simply add *d* or *ed* to any present verb to form the past tense. They have figured out that English has patterns; they just don't know the exceptions yet. Don't use "comed" ("came"), "knowed" ("knew"), "runned" ("ran"), "seed" ("saw"), or "sweeped" ("swept").

How far did the Herdegens **fly?** (*Not*, **fly?**. —see page 161.)

If you're unsure about a verb form, check a dictionary. Some examples:

Look up "burst" and you'll see "burst/burst/burst," so you know you can't say, "The sumo wrestler **bursted** into tears." Make it "burst."

Don't say "I **drug** my desk across the room." ("Drag" is a regular verb: drag, dragging, dragged, dragged.) Make it "dragged."

Use "learned," not "learnt."

ZITS by Jerry Scott and Jim Borgman

Here's a sampling of the more than two hundred irregular verbs:

Present Tense	Present Participle	Past Tense (no helping verb)	Past Participle (needs helping verb—has, have, had)
am, is, are (to be)	being	was, were	been
arise	arising	arose	arisen
beat	beating	beat	beaten
become	becoming	became	become
bite	biting	bit	bitten, bit
blow	blowing	blew	blown
break	breaking	broke	broken
bring	bringing	brought (never "brang" or "brung")	brought (never "brang" or "brung")
burn	burning	burned*	burned*
cast	casting	cast (never "casted"; but "broadcast" or "broadcasted")	cast (never "casted"; but "broadcast" or "broadcasted")
choose	choosing	chose	chosen
cling	clinging	clung	clung

*You may see "burnt" as an adjective: burnt syrup.

Rusty **brought** a bag of mail. (*Not,* **brang**—see above.)

Present Tense	Present Participle	Past Tense	Past Participle
come	coming	came	come
cost	costing	cost	cost
do	doing	did	done
dream	dreaming	dreamed, dreamt	dreamed, dreamt
drive	driving	drove	driven
eat	eating	ate	eaten
feed	feeding	fed	fed
fight	fighting	fought	fought
find	finding	found	found
flee	fleeing	fled	fled
forgive	forgiving	forgave	forgiven
freeze	freezing	froze	frozen
give	giving	gave	given
go	going	went	gone
grow	growing	grew	grown
hang (execute)	hanging	hanged	hanged
hang (suspend)	hanging	hung	hung
hide	hiding	hid	hidden
hold	holding	held	held
kneel	kneeling	knelt	knelt
know	knowing	knew	known
leave	leaving	left	left
lose	losing	lost	lost
made	making	made	made
meet	meeting	met	met
plead	pleading	pleaded, pled	pleaded, pled
prove	proving	proved	proved, proven
put	putting	put	put
run	running	ran	run
say	saying	said	said
see	seeing	saw (*never* "seen")	seen
set	setting	set	set
sew	sewing	sewed	sewn, sewed
shake	shaking	shook	shaken
shine	shining	shone (the sun shone)	shone (the sun has shone)
		shined (he shined shoes)	shined (he has shined shoes)
show	showing	showed	shown

A pair of vultures **swoops** in! (*Not,* **swoop**—see page 51.)

Present Tense	Present Participle	Past Tense	Past Participle
sing	singing	sang	sung
sink	sinking	sank	sunk
slide	sliding	slid	slid
sneak	sneaking	sneaked (*never* "snuck")	sneaked (*never* "snuck")
speak	speaking	spoke	spoken
spring	springing	sprang	sprung
sting	stinging	stung (*never* "stang")	stung (*never* "stang")
swear	swearing	swore	sworn
swim	swimming	swam	swum
swing	swinging	swung	swung
tear (*rhymes with "air"*)	tearing	tore	torn
think	thinking	thought	thought
throw	throwing	threw	thrown
wake	waking	woke, waked	waked, woken
wring	wringing	wrung	wrung
write	writing	wrote	written

Quick Verb Review

Remember—past-tense verbs (third column) stand alone: They don't have helping verbs. Past participles of verbs (fourth column) *must* have a helping verb.

Say, "came" or "had come"; "saw" or "had seen"; "sank" or "have sunk"; "ate" or "have eaten". Don't say, "had came," "had saw," "have sank," or "have ate."

> **We saw** the Lipizzaner horse show at the fair. (*Not,* **We seen.**)

> They **had gone** to see *Pearl Harbor.* (*Not,* **had went.**)

"To Be" Verbs (*See verbs of being, page 208.*)

Verb Mood (*See mood, page 196.*)

Verbals (*See gerund, page 191; infinitives, page 192; and participles, page 200.*) Besides having forms that show tense, mood, person, voice, and number, verbs can take three forms: gerunds, infinitives, and participles. These "verbals" don't act as the main verb of a sentence. Instead, they take on new roles as nouns, adjectives, or adverbs. Verbals can take direct and indirect objects.

> Great Aunt Izzy's doing **well.** (*Not,* **good**—see page 19.)

Verbing

"Verbing" means turning other parts of speech into verbs. The word "verbing" itself is an example of this, and a term we use here with tongue fully in cheek.

> Hurricane Opal will **landfall** by daybreak.

> Hermione **googled** Ron on the Internet.

Sometimes "verbed" words work their way into speech, writing, and, eventually, dictionaries. Others don't.

Many words that began life as nouns are now commonly accepted as verbs: *to jackhammer, to water ski, to premiere, to mainstream, to diagnose* (from diagnosis), *to author,* and *to host.*

Some dictionaries even recognize "to calendar," but the Grammar Patrol loathes this one! And "to calendarize" is even more odious!

The "verbing" of words such as "access" and "impact" bothers many people. Other words, like "overnight" and "jury," seem on their way to becoming verbs.

SINGLE SLICES by Peter Kohlsaat

© 1998 Los Angeles Times Syndicate

Access

"Access," although now listed as a verb in dictionaries, remains controversial. Hearing "access" used as a verb is still hard for many people to take!

> He'll gain **access** (noun) to dating services worldwide.

> "Please wait while we **access** (verb) your entire life history."

Impact

Help the Grammar Patrol hold the line against using "impact" as a verb:

> How will Farnsworth's news **impact** the Wutherspoon account?

This asks, "How will Farnsworth's news **affect** the Wutherspoon account?"

Have you seen *Who Framed Roger **Rabbit**? (Not, **Rabbit??** —see page 163.)

If that's what you mean, why not use "affect?"

Your safest bet is to use "impact" as the powerful noun (meaning "strong influence" or "collision") that it is:

We recognize the **impact** of Morris Dees's work for tolerance.

You even need to take care in using "impact" as a noun. Where "impact" is used to mean the noun "effect," or the verb "affect," why not use those words?

Mama Mia's new garlic-jalapeño sauce had a negative **effect** (*not* **impact**) on sales.

The new garlic-jalapeño sauce negatively **affected** (*not* **impacted**) Mama Mia's sales.

Overnight

You might once have sent jewels **overnight** (an adverb) or by **overnight** express (an adjective). Today, you can say, "**Overnight** the jewels to London." This is easily understood, even though "overnight" is not yet officially a verb.

Jury

Some dictionaries acknowledge "jury" as a noun (twelve on a **jury**), an adjective (a **juried** art show), and a verb. Other dictionaries don't yet list "jury" as a verb, as it's used here:

Catherine **juried** the Park Point Art Exhibit.

Will "jury" officially be accepted as a verb? Stay tuned to the amazing world of "verbing."

Verbing *Can* Work

Sometimes turning nouns to verbs is just common sense. Like "overnight," above, the new words "email" and "fax" (from "facsimile") are now commonly used as verbs.

I'll **email** you.

Fax me your résumé.

Informally, people use the names of companies as verbs, too.

I'll **FedEx** or **UPS** you the drafts.

Xerox this fast!

Extensive searches **were** conducted. (*Not*, **was**—see page 26.)

Verbing Can Mangle Meaning

Beware of gratuitous "verbing." These give the Grammar Patrol the shivers:

A store's new motto: A new way to **coupon**!

Radio ad: We're **efforting** to serve you better.

Magazine ad: With a Web site, a company has a much better chance of **impressioning** its customers.

"I **office** at Danny's Coffee Shop."

English evolves, but be a word watcher. Is the "verbed" word a sensible addition to our language, or is it nonsensical?

Verb Phrases

A verb phrase is a group of words that functions like a verb.
(In Grammarspeak, it can also be called a "simple predicate.")

> **has crept**   **is being teleported**   **might have been watered**

Verbs of Being

The term "verbs of being" simply refers to "to be" verbs: *am, is, are, was, were, be, been, being.*

Voice, Active and Passive

Verbs can be active or passive. In the **active voice**, the subject performs the action. Headlines always use the active voice: "Yankees **Win** Series," *not* "Series **Won by** Yankees."

> Andy **spotted** the tornado from ten miles away.
> (*active verb*)

In the **passive voice**, the subject receives the action or is acted upon:

> The walleye **was caught** by Herbie.
> (*passive verb*)

Key words can indicate the passive voice: Be on the lookout for "by," "to," and "for" when they follow "was," "were," and "will be."

> **was hit by**   **were sent to**   **will be used for**

Most writing calls for the active voice. It's clear, direct, and takes fewer words than the passive. The exceptions are scientific, medical, or formal writing where using the passive voice is appropriate and may even work

The **number** of termites is rising. (*Not,* **amount**—see page 28.)

better.

A grammar checker would flag many passive verbs in Abraham Lincoln's famous "Gettysburg Address." Mr. Lincoln's words remain moving as written.

(Whew! That's it for the verb section, grammar lovers.)

VICE, VISE

A "vice" is "a bad habit." A "vise" is a tool with jaws that clamp.

Onion rings are Laverne's favorite **vice**.

My head feels as if it's caught in a **vise**.

VOICE, ACTIVE AND PASSIVE *(See verbs, page 208.)*

VOWELS *(See consonants, vowels, page 64.)*

YOUR, YOU'RE

"Your" is a possessive pronoun—it shows ownership.

I love **your** new plaid socks.

Send in **your** Halloween Jell-O recipe by March 1.

"You're" is the contraction of "you are."

You're welcome to my go-cart. ("You are" welcome.)

If you can you read this bumper sticker, **you're** too close. ("You are" too close.)

TIP: "Your" is often mistaken for "you're." Test to see if you've chosen the correct spelling by substituting "you are." If it fits, the spelling should be "you're."

He's more diplomatic than **I**. (*Not*, **me**—see page 156.)

MORE GRAMMAR RESOURCES

Great grammar resources abound. Check your library, bookstore, and online sites to further explore the ins and outs of English grammar.

The American Heritage Dictionary of the English Language, 4th ed., New York: Houghton Mifflin, 2000.

Agnes, Michael E., editor, *Webster's New World Misspeller's Dictionary,* 2nd ed., Indiana, IN: Wiley Publishers, Inc., 1997.

Bear, Donald R., et al. *Words Their Way: Word Study for Phonics, Vocabulary, and Spelling Instruction.* New York: Prentice Hall, 1995.

Bruder, Mary Newton. *Much Ado About a Lot: How to Mind Your Manners in Print and in Person.* New York: Hyperion, 2000.

The Chicago Manual of Style: The Essential Guide for Writers, Editors, and Publishers, 15th ed., John Grossman (preface), Chicago, IL: University of Chicago Press, 2003.

Elster, Charles Harrington, *The Big Book of Beastly Mispronunciations*, New York: Houghton Mifflin Company, 1999.

Fine, Edith H., and Judith P. Josephson. *Nitty-Gritty Grammar: A Not-So-Serious Guide to Clear Communication.* Berkeley, Calif.: Ten Speed Press, 1998.

Garner, Bryan A., *A Dictionary of Modern American Usage,* New York: Oxford University Press, 1998.

Gordon, Karen Elizabeth, *The New Well-Tempered Sentence: A Punctuation Handbook for the Innocent, the Eager, and the Doomed,* New York: Ticknor & Fields, 1993.

Hodges, John C., et al., *Hodges' Harbrace Handbook,* 14th ed., New York: Harcourt College Publishers 2001.

Lederer, Richard, and Richard Dowis. *Sleeping Dogs Don't Lay.* New York: St. Martin's Press, 2001.

O'Conner, Patricia T. *Woe Is I,* New York: Riverhead Books, 1998.

Publication Manual of the American Psychological Association, 5th ed. Washington, D.C.: American Psychological Association, 2001.

Sabin, William A. *The Gregg Reference Manual,* 10th ed. New York: McGraw Hill/Irwin, 2004.

Stilman, Anne. *Grammatically Correct: The Writer's Essential Guide to Punctuation, Spelling, Style, Usage and Grammar. Cincinnati,* Ohio: Writer's Digest Books, 1997.

Strumpf, Michael, and Auriel Douglas, *The Grammar Bible: Everything You Always Wanted to Know about Grammar but Didn't Know Whom to Ask,* New York: Owl Books, 2004.

Strunk, William Jr., and E. B. White. *The Elements of Style,* 4th ed. New York: Longman, 2000.

Venolia, Jan, *Write Right!: A Desktop Digest of Punctuation, Grammar, and Style,* 4th ed., Berkeley, CA: Ten Speed Press, 2001.

Wallraff, Barbara. *Word Court: Wherein verbal virtue is rewarded, crimes against the language are punished, and poetic justice is done.* New York: Harcourt, 2000.

Webster's New World Misspeller's Dictionary. Foster City, Calif.: IDG Books Worldwide, 1997.

For more on words and grammar, consult the sagacious reference librarians at your local library and surf the Net for grammar tips. Google sticky grammar topics for specific information.

ABOUT THE AUTHORS

Photo by Bob Bretell

Grammar is a very serious business.
—The Grammar Patrol

Judith Pinkerton Josephson (left) and Edith Hope Fine (right), aka the Grammar Patrol, taught grammar with a comic twist through San Diego State University Extension for twenty years. They have close to thirty books between them. Both are ardent bibliophiles and spot grammar bloopers everywhere.

Judith, an avid swimmer and cook, plays the violin. She has written poetry and nonfiction, including biographies about Beethoven, Walt Disney, Nikki Giovanni, Jesse Owen, Allan Pinkerton (no relation!), and Mother Jones. Her three childhood history books focus on the pioneer era, the turn of the century (the early1900s), and World War II.

Edith, a rabid recycler, likes swimming and Sudoku. Her books include *CryptoMania!: Teleporting into Greek and Latin with the CryptoKids*, *Under the Lemon Moon*, and biographies of Gary Paulsen, Barbara McClintock, Rosa Parks, and Martin Luther King Jr. Her Greek/Latin CryptoKids Decoder Program is used in schools nationwide.

Besides *Nitty-Gritty Grammar* and *More Nitty-Gritty Grammar*, Fine and Josephson are coauthors of two other books. Fine and Josephson both live in southern California near their families. Visit their websites for grammar quizzes, book giveaways, and more:

www.grammarpatrol.com
www.judithjosephson.com

www.cryptokids.com
www.edithfine.com

INDEX

213